QUARTER-MILE

The Drag Racing Book
for Spectators and Competitors

STEVEN MYATT

The Drag Racing Book
for Spectators and Competitors

MRP

MOTOR RACING PUBLICATIONS LTD
28 Devonshire Road, Chiswick, London W4 2HD, England

ISBN 0 900549 65 3

First published 1982

Photosetting by Strewlight Ltd., London W1
Monochrome origination by The Purchasing Link Ltd., Warlingham, Surrey
Cover design by Jack Andrews
Printed in Great Britain by Page Bros. (Norwich) Ltd., Norwich, Norfolk

The Credits

Very many thanks for his help, advice, proof-reading and priceless friendship must go firstly to Dennis Foy – who not only planned the book's structure but also suffered over-sweetened tea and sticky puns with great tolerance.

Particular thanks, too, to: Steven and Leone Murty, John Revill, Paul Hogarth and Tony Murray of the Pennine Drag Racing Club; Margaret Warne and Paul Garland of the BDRA; Baz Barron, Alan Wigmore and Frances Parker of the NDRC; Pip Higham and Tony Howarth of the Village Bike Shop; Mike Key; Ron Clarke; Frank Hedley of Removatop; Dave Grady of Super Power USA; Barry Reynolds, who administers Ford UK's press fleet; Bosse Lindstrom of Bosse Buss; Chuck Rudy of Sellersville PA for the Stateside truck shots; Dave Hamill for reading, correcting and suggesting; and Chris Mossop for the graphics.

This book is dedicated to Judy and Glacier Mint; and they know why. Thank you.

S.M.

CONTENTS

In Stage: INTRODUCTION   7

Diggers and Blowers, Floppers and Cherries: BORN IN AMERICA   11

Coming Together: THE BRITISH CLUBS   21
        British Drag Racing Association
        National Drag Racing Club
        Pennine Drag Racing Club

Class Distinction: THE RACE CLASSES   33
        Dragster
        Funny Car
        Competition Altered
        Modified
        Production
        Street/Roadster

Pumping Rubber: BRACKET RACING   55

Chain Reaction: BIKE DRAGGING   59

Staging, Holeshooting, Shifting and Shutdowns: RACE PROCEDURE   67

Strip Life: DAYS IN THE DRAG RACING SCENE   74

Dreams of Glory: WHAT TO BUY AND RACE   81

Bound for Glory: BUILDING A BRACKET BOMBER/
            STREET CLASS CAR   87

Bolt-on Survival: SAFETY SYSTEMS   117

Don't Pick the Cherries: WHAT TO TAKE TO THE STRIP   123

You Hot Rod Heroes: RACING YOUR CUSTOM MACHINE   126

Taking the Strain: SPONSORSHIP   131

Dream Teams and Clean Machines: TEAM IDENTITY   135

Off the Rails: SHOWMANSHIP   139

All The World's In Stage: DRAGGING IN EUROPE   145

Drag Dictionary: JARGON EXPLAINED   149

Red Light Districts: GUIDE TO CLUBS AND STRIPS   155

Shutdown: SPECIALIST SUPPLIERS   158

Sylvia Hauser picks up the ex-Rossi Dodge Challenger and heads for home. The car is still in its original colours, just as it came from the United States.

It is possible to run a street and strip car. Neon Star, from South London, is a regular contender at Santa Pod Raceway, but is seen here pulling glances on the Chelsea Cruise.

In Stage

INTRODUCTION

No other area of motor sport, when you come to think about it, really makes as much sense as drag racing. In the normal run of things, very few of us thunder through Welsh forests on unmade roads in imminent danger of spinning off on a corner and wrapping ourselves round a nearby pine. Nor, come to that, are any of us used to screaming through the side streets of Monaco at 160 mph without, at least, demolishing a few souvenir shops and dipping moistly into the harbour. Drag racing, on the other hand, makes sense. Excepting geriatics, guys with their mother-in-law in the back seat and Reliant Robin owners, the spirit of dragging can be seen at any set of traffic lights you care to name. Who doesn't look across at his neighbour's car as he waits on a red, and then try to beat him to the next set? That, in essence, is drag racing.

A more precise definition of the sport would be that it is a test of acceleration across a measured quarter of a mile from a standing start, where the first car to cross the finish line is the winner. It really is as simple as that.

Organized drag racing has been flourishing at club levels in Europe for about two decades, but the spirit of the sport has been around since the word car became plural. Europe's first drag race probably took place in the last decade of the 19th century, the contestants sitting high above their wooden-spoked road wheels and tiller steering in their Panhard-Levassors or De Dion Boutons. We don't know who won or what his time was, but I wouldn't be at all surprised if there was money on the outcome.

This book cannot answer all the questions about the sport, nor is it an objective and scholarly thesis; but it does try to show as full a picture as possible of dragging in the Eighties and the world which surrounds it. Whether you are a dedicated fan, are participating in the sport at lower levels, or are simply interested and would like to move further in, then this is for you. You will find that I assume an interest to take part rather than just spectate — if only because it makes more sense to speak from the start line than from the back of the spectator banking — but I do hope that you will appreciate your day at the races all the more with the information and explanations this book provides.

From time to time I move from 'I' to 'we' in the text. This means The Press Gang Drag Race Team — myself and Dennis Foy (currently Features Editor of *Hot Car* magazine) — which is best known for rather unimpressive appearances in other people's machines. The team's milestone, though, is Dennis' tough but dinky 3-litre V6-powered 100E racer.

My credentials for writing this book must start with having been a founder member of the Rainy City Cruisers, having worked on the *Rod and Custom Shows,* and having been Features Editor of *Custom Car* magazine for two and a half years. I have written for many motoring publications and my first book, *The Complete Customiser,* was published in 1980. That, at least, is the *curriculum vitae* — what counts for more is a first-hand knowledge of what it feels like to sit at the line watching for the christmas tree flashing into life,

Dutchman Henk Vink is the fastest European on two wheels and runs 7s on his double-engined Kawasaki.

the chats and laughs in the pits, and the sights and smells which have illuminated my attendance at British strips over the last five years.

Drag racing is an exciting and challenging sport; it's about straightforward do-or-die competition. It's fast and dramatic; and both victory and defeat are sudden and final. It's not a sport for the slow-witted. the indecisive, or the faint-hearted — it is, however, for the bold, the dedicated, the cool-headed . . . and the young. To race a drag car is to accept that you may be driving hundreds of miles to a strip, you may have spent a lot of money and a lot more time on the car, you may have had a week of sleepless nights, you may be plagued with external problems and holdups — and then, after no more than 12 seconds of competition, you may well be beaten by a better driver in a better car. Or worse, blow your own motor. The only permissible reaction then is a determination to be back for the next meeting with a faster or better-built car — bound for vengeance.

Drag racing is an excellent motor sport from a spectator's point of view, for many reasons. Most importantly, you are able to see the entire race and all the action from a single vantage point. There's none of this business of seeing a car zip past and then having to wait several minutes to glimpse it again. In dragging, you see the cars start and then see one guy win and the other guy lose. There's a lot of 'theatre' in drag racing, too; not only the sights — hefty burnouts and frantic crews pushing spitting cars back to the line in time to stage, but also the sounds — crackling funny cars and burbling street muscle, and then the smell — burning rubber and the heady whiffs of nitro fumes. And there is one more element — something that comes out of the fact that there are just two guys out there, alone, doing battle. It's like gladiators or knights jousting. It's something to do with the most basic gut-level instincts of competition — and this is where personalities start to crop up, grudge races begin, and the ability to 'out-psych' your opponent can win you a race even before the lights have started coming down the christmas tree.

European drag racing has come too far over the past decade and a half for me to try to combine Europe and America in this book. Much as I'd like the US sales, things are different, so this is a non-American drag racing book.

A brace of Comp Altered Pops on the line. Such machinery proves that you don't need megabuck rails to either compete or please the crowd.

The Swedes tend to do things properly when it comes to drag racing. Although they are short on strips they're a major force in the sport.

To some degree, also, it is written for the unconverted, or at least, in a way that the unconverted can easily understand. Jargon needs explaining, so if your name is Nobbie or Bootsie please bear with me. Throughout the book I do tend to speak of drag racers as males. This is mere convenience, because there are more ladies positively participating in drag racing than in any other motor sport I can think of — in England alone, Sue Coles, Liz Burn, Roz Prior, Shellie Billington, Sylvia Hauser, Jean Tidswell and Hazel Wlosek all spring quickly to mind — let alone Leone Murty, who frequently drives Pennine's wheelie car. Forgive me for saying 'he' rather than 'he or she' all the time . . .

It is quite impossible to predict the future for drag racing. Over the past few years, external events have created chaos in the Western World in all forms of motoring and motor sport. Dragging depends on fuel — though, of course, it uses far less fuel than most other forms of car racing — and political actions could bring unforseen restrictions. Nothing else can stunt the rise of drag racing in Europe, though. It's too exciting, too much of a real good time, and too close to so many hearts for it to do anything but mushroom in popularity. Come the day when petrol is rationed to a gallon per person per week there'll be many of us who will ride to the strip on horseback and pool our coupons so that the racers may race. There is, after all, nothing else in this world quite like a warm and lazy summer afternoon spent beside a rumbling quarter-mile.

Diggers and Blowers, Floppers and Cherries

BORN IN AMERICA

High summer in 1950, hot, very hot, the air quite still and the heat bouncing back up off the roads and sidewalks of Santa Ana, Southern California. The grey and sprawling conurbation of Los Angeles lies to the north, to the south-west are the vast surf-thundering sea-beaches of Huntington — not 10 miles distant — Newport and Laguna; away to the east the mountains rise into the pale-to-deep mid-blue sky — out towards Corona and Elsinore. Southern California funnels itself into a beautiful narrow strip, its wealth exaggerated by the compression; the Pacific squeezes from one side and the high arid deserts squeeze from the other.

Five years are long enough for the Second World War to be little more than a memory. This new land has no time for the indulgence of reflection. There are no physical scars to jar the memory; war widows, orphans, the crippled are very few in number to any European comparison. No bombs fell on Glendale or Burbank, no-one ever really expected the Germans or the Japanese to start landing their infantry on the hot golden SoCal beaches. The war oiled the cogs of industry; brought jobs and dollars; united the populace and helped fuse immigrants into Americans. And the momentum, now, is sustained. In Europe they are still rationing food, buying extra petrol at black-market prices, trying to find work for demobbed veterans and rebuilding their homes and churches and lives.

Southern California, though, is devouring air-conditioning units, chest freezers, electric toasters and huge twin-tub washing machines with an impressive greed. The ads in the *National Geographic* promise holidays in Hawaii, 35-foot cabin cruisers for manual workers, curving swimming pools and half a dozen acres of landscaped gardens for the professional classes. These Southern Californians — after an evening watching Lucille Ball on TV, Roller Derby downtown, or Bette Davis in *All About Eve* at the drive-in — they rest easy in their beds; the leaders are so solid, so American — Truman in the White House, Allen Dulles at the CIA, Joseph McCarthy at the House Committee on UnAmerican Activities. Joe Louis is still supreme in the ring, and General MacArthur, out in the Far East in early July, is supremely confident that he would need no more than a week to settle the little local difficulty in Korea.

Not everyone can afford a Cadillac, sure — at prices starting around $5,000 — but the affordable range in the showrooms would stagger a European. There's a new low-price Mercury sports coupe as well as their Monterey with its padded vinyl roof. Not as pretty, but lighter and faster — the Oldsmobile 88 with its Rocket V8 and a neat 135 bhp. Dodge? Plymouth? All within the family's reach. Chevrolet? In 1950 they'll produce more than two million units.

That's something else, though — that's only the showroom world. Out here, a few miles outside town, today's the day; on the broad concrete runways of Orange County Airport it's the inaugural meeting of the world's first commercially-run drag strip.

It owes its existence to a trio of under-capitalized *entrepreneurs* and a whole legion of wild young bucks with high-spirited motor cars. The guys themselves are really neat. Lean and lithe, tanned and cool — they wear a uniform of baggy blue-black jeans with deep turnups and narrow belts, plain white T-shirt, white socks and clip-on sneakers, a vaguely GI crew-cut . . . oh, and shades. They are *neat*. They lolly-lolly around, swagger and bluff, keeping cool, telling the jokes they can't tell in the dining room at home, laughing and sparring; white teeth and gold-plate identity bracelets.

The introduction of commerce — and all that it can bring — is an understandable turning point for any new-found sport. It's the move from competitors watching competitors to the creation of a spectator crowd; the introspection must end and the paying public must be enticed in.

Not that you'd really know it today, though. A few friends are here and standing loosely around. Difficult, really, to tell the spectators from the competitors. Seems a gregarious sport. Any number of guys cluster round a car; there are cut-down raunchy race cars in a variety of styles — hi-boy fenderless roadsters and prewar coupes, mostly three-windowed, chopped, stripped, louvred and with nothing in the way of fancy paint or fey cosmetics. Street cars, these — every one the veteran of a score of traffic tickets and a weekly run-in with the cops.

The measured strip is three-tenths of a mile long and bumpy and the racers' terminal speeds are computed by a neat light-beam-trip system. The starter has put on a white shirt and white pants for the occasion; one, he's going to play marshal today and make the most of it, and two, the better racers can see him the better his chances of survival. No christmas tree lights. The starter stands a couple of yards beyond the start line, between the paths of the two cars, and beckons them forward. They roll up towards him. If he decides that they're rolling about level as they near the line, he does his little jump into the air, tucks his legs right up underneath, and brings his flag down in a long arc as though he's carving someone up with a battle axe. The cars have roared and dusted past him long before he's recovered his feet, and are halfway down the strip before he's recovered his balance. Observers at the finish line decide the winner and signal with more waving flags. Next pair, please.

So the guys keep coming around, returning down the back, parking up in the pit area. The car-club guys get out their spanners and fiddle — some changing plugs to try it a little hotter maybe, a few working harder and with greater necessity. Mostly, though, they just lolly-lolly around; light up a Lucky Strike and punch shoulders and watch the racing. It's all a hell of a lot better than the usual routine.

Club strips are rare. The Timing Association have to find a runway or something, negotiate like mad, wear a collar and tie, keep referring to 'the committee' and utterly deny any connection with the hooligans who've made Riverside Road unsafe for old ladies and Hudsons after midnight on Saturdays — and then repeat the process downtown to get a permit from the Chief of Police. It's all possible, sure, but a real sweat.

Much easier — much more natural maybe — for the guys simply to cruise over to Riverside Road late on Saturday . . . or the fireroads, or the flood-channels . . . all depends how quickly the prowl cars are responding to complaints from outraged but upright citizens.

Fierce racing. The drag marked by guesswork and illuminated by the headlights of two rows of parked cars. The starter might use a handkerchief for a flag, do the little jump and simply wave his arm, or flash on a torch; then the gravel flies up and the rods hurtle away — real seat-of-the-pants midnight street racing.

Been going on since the Twenties, this, long enough for myths and heroes to emerge. Back then, the vast majority of Californians were first generation immigrants. Europe was traumatized by the aftermath of its First World War, and as more Europeans landed at Ellis Island, more and more families were moving west across the continent. Chasing promises, looking for an El Dorado. And the best way to go was by Model T Ford. By 1927 Ford had produced more than 15 million Model Ts and, frighteningly over-laden with children, chattels, rocking chairs and Momma's ivory-handled cutlery

A typical Stateside combination of the old and the new. This is George Montgomery with his 1937 Willys coupe, powered by a blown Chevrolet and equipped with automatic transmission.

Out comes the chute as the Stellings and Hampshire dragster completes another fast run on a Californian strip.

service, many of them were eased westwards between the wars. Shacks sprung up where a T had expired; small towns grew up in the Mid-West when the family's resolution had given out even before the T had.

The new life was hard, but the rewards *were* there. There was also any number of old Model Ts for the kids to get their hands on. It was no big deal to strip off virtually all the bodywork and all unnecessary ancillaries to end up with a lighter, sleeker and unnervingly stark racer. Hop-up engine conversions were available from a surprisingly early date; but bought-in spares aside, most kids simply took the car and engine apart to find out how it worked — and how to make it go faster. These 'buckboard' Ts were then coaxed into all sorts of mad antics, to give momentum to the evolutionary process of many forms of motor racing. Mostly it was for fun, nothing more. Up in the mountains, though, the young bucks and their buckboards were a part of the family's cottage industry — moonshine booze. The kids were draymen — the delivery drivers — and they had to keep their buckboard Ts that little bit faster than the federal excise agents in *their* Model Ts.

The potential of the T was always limited. The introduction of the Ford Model A, the Model B and, in 1932, the flathead 3.6-litre V8, must have been highspots in the young lives of many teenage kids, and it wasn't long before the new styles and the new engines filtered down to the hot-rod boys.

Ford were the brand leaders in motor cars for some time, but there were many others, like Graham, Reo and Franklin, and better-known names such as Plymouth, Chevrolet and Chrysler. The manufacturers churned out their produce as fast as they could; in 1934 Chevrolet's vehicle production numbered 1,275,000 units and over their first 23 years in existence they had made 10 million cars. The sheer availability of cheap cars allowed the kids not only to race their street cars, but also to afford race-only machines. From early on it wasn't too rare to find a high school guy with indulgent parents who had a true race car to his name, for stock car racing, hill-climbing, lakes racing — whatever. Lakes? Lakes — dried up lakes, especially the salt flats such as Bonneville. These provided a reasonably flat and virtually endless sheer surface for some very hairy high-speed flat-out racing as well as for world land speed records. From the Timing Associations which organized the lakes racing sprang the organization which we would recognize today as the foundation of formal drag racing.

Not only was lakes racing about getting the maximum return from the car's engine — and speeds over 150 mph were reached quite soon — but the fundamental principles of streamlining were being applied, so that the power of the engine could be put to the most good.

In the late-Twenties, a scientific researcher by the name of Glen Curtis took a stock five-window coupe, which could manage 74 mph, and turned the bodyshell right round; with the better curves cutting through the air it now touched 87 mph. He then went on to add a 1,500-lb teardrop-shaped trailer — and although the coupe's weight was doubled, its performance was increased by 11 per cent. Norman Bel Geddes took the theme further by designing a complete teardrop car in 1931 which, with rear engine and rear-wheel drive, would have carried eight people in great space within its conventionally-proportioned 116-inch wheelbase. Drag-coefficient factors are only becoming really important to the motor manufacturers today — 50 years on. The ideas, however, caught on very quickly with those looney kids hurtling ever quicker across the salt flats.

Building a really aerodynamically efficient body needed both research and money — but why go through all that when Uncle Sam seems perfectly prepared to do the work for you? Military aircraft of the time carried 'drop' fuel tanks — long teardrop-shaped tanks which were slung under the wings and could be discarded when empty or in the case of emergency. It wasn't long before the first lakes/drag car appeared clothed in a superbly-aerodynamic ex-USAAF drop tank. After the war these drop or 'belly' tanks weren't too hard to find, and guys like Tom Beatty were popping up all over — he built his blown 258-cubic inch flathead-engined belly tanker in his Sun Valley speed shop and took it to 211 mph. The shape of modern dragsters was evolving.

All of which, in fact, takes us a step or two beyond that sweaty day in 1950 at the newly-founded Orange County Raceway. Not only did the founding of Orange County bring new faces and new money to the sport, it also helped to establish drag racing as a true branch of motor sport —moving it away from lakes racing and the rest. The following year saw the birth of what was to become the sport's governing body — the National Hot Rod Assosciation. The Editor of *Hot Rod* magazine, Wally Parks, was elected as the first President, with Akton Miller as Vice President and Marvin Lee as Secretary. The NHRA's slogan was 'Dedicated To Safety' and they started a prudent PR campaign to rid themselves of the animosity caused in many places by the midnight street racers. The NHRA also laid down the first set of mandatory strip measurements. The strip was to be exactly 1,320 feet long (a quarter of a mile) within a paved area no less than 3,500 feet long and 60 feet wide. As well as safety distances for the spectators and all sorts of advice and regulations for both racers and race promoters, the Association laid down that the car's terminal speed was to be measured across the 132 feet-long 'traps' which straddle the finish lane so that, by taking an average, they might obtain the truest across-the-line speeds. (ETs —elapsed times — now rated all-important, were not considered until much later when more advanced electronics made the instant read-out of a precise time possible and the emphasis gradually shifted.)

The NHRA also laid down the sport's basic classes, eight in all, though each with a number of sub-divisions based on the car's weight computed against its cubic capacity, except for the lowest class, Stock, where the car's 'shipping weight' was divided by its 'advertised horsepower'. The original classes were Stock (S), Gas (G) — coupes and sedans, Street Roadsters (SR), Altereds (A) — coupes and sedans, Roadsters (R), Modified Roadsters (MR), Competition (C) — coupes and sedans, and Dragsters (D). They got round the classification problem of dual-engined and supercharged cars by simply moving both into the next higher class.

The original identification system largely holds true today (though the ratios have altered); the original rules had Dragsters split into three groups, Class A being cars with up to 3.99 lb weight for every cubic inch of engine displacement, Class B being 4.00 to 5.59 per cubic inch and Class C 5.60 lb and over per cubic inch. The car's identity tag would be its number followed by its sub-division and class, A/D for example, denoting Dragster class, top sub-division.

The Fifties was a decade of expansion and rapid progress in dragging. By 1958 there were more cars on the San Bernardino freeway in the rush-hour than in the whole of Asia and South America, Orange County Raceway was now far from being the only commercial strip but was prospering indeed, and the Frank/Harryman/Brown blown-Olds rail was running 157.61 mph (10.10 seconds) on nothing more than petrol and representing a total investment of only $3,000.

The class structure had by then played a large part in formulating the shape and physical appearance of drag cars, and the development along recognizable lines was advancing steadily. Drop tanks had long since been discarded and the principles of aerodynamics had been greatly refined. Narrowed rear axles allowed Dragsters to present a much smaller front elevation and thus reduce their drag coefficients further. Masters Auto Supply built a totally enclosed aluminium-bodied D/C Dragster which, powered by a four-carb 283 from a '55 Chevy, ran 132 mph over a quarter. Bob Zeller and Don Johnson used a similar styling theme, but made their Dragster's body out of glass-fibre; with power from a '56 Buick V8 breathing through a six-pack, they ran the quarter to reach 137.20 mph.

Specialist services were no problems. Speed equipment companies such as Iskenderian, Crane, Pink, Ansen and M & H were well-established. There were chassis builders, engine builders and transmission builders. Although banned for a few years by the NHRA at the end of the decade, 'fuel' was available — alcohol and nitro mostly, though various home-made cocktails burned out many an engine. Fuel injection was popular — Hilborn could offer applications for everything from old flatheads to the latest Chrysler or

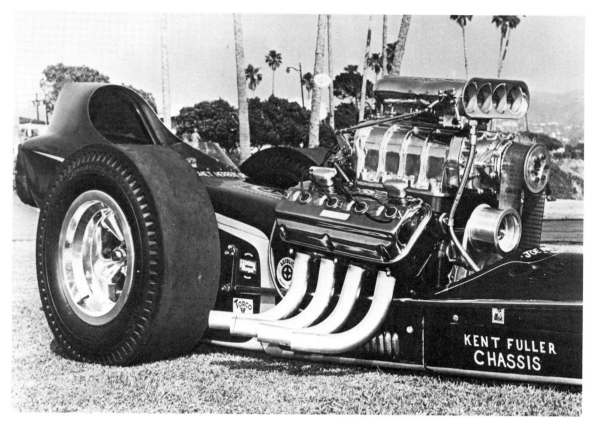

Typical of the high standard of presentation seen in US drag racing and emulated in Europe. Gleaming in the sun is the blown 6.8-litre Chrysler V8 of the Stellings and Hampshire dragster pictured in the mid-Sixties.

Dodge mill. For Dragsters, though, supercharging was really getting to be *the* thing. The short-lived fashion for blowers to be located ahead of the engine at that time, rather than above it, depended on the Potvin mounting kit; the McCullochs and the GMCs were both bulky units which operated by linear 1:1 drive to the crankshaft, whereas the SCOT blower sat on top between the rocker covers (allowing the possibility of over or under-driving) with the carbs or injectors on top. Ted Rawleigh eased 670 bhp out of his double-blown Hilborn-injected Oldsmobile V8, and that in turn, with 33 per cent nitro, took his rail to 155 mph . . . though at a total cost reputed to have been around $10,000.

In the main, the old-type coupes and roadsters dominated the sport's middle classes — and just kept getting faster. The Comp Altered style developed from Thirties Plymouth coupes in trad style and the like. Such smaller, lighter cars obviously started their dragging lives at a considerable advantage, and the smaller late-model machines became popular for the same reason. Crosleys, for example, were tiny shopping cars for the (comparatively) poor, and a fair number of the '48/'49 models were eventually stripped and re-engined and taken dragging. Archy Ary chopped and channelled his '49 Crosley sedan, spent most of his $3,700 budget on the six-pack '57 Chrysler engine and took the Altered to 140.53 mph at Colton Drag Strip; it was quite typical of the breed.

Street machinery, running in Stock and the new class of Super Stock at the bottom of the scale, was by no means left behind. They benefited enormously from the manufacturers' performance race of the late-Fifties. Having vied with each other to win customers with styling changes for many years, Detroit began to emphasize and increase their cars' power outputs. There was optional fuel injection on the '57 Corvette, the Paxton blower for the Thunderbird, the one-bhp-per-cubic-inch 283 which powered the Chevy Bel Airs in '57, and even stock six-seat Buick Centurys were running sub-10-second 0-60s. Given such a good base, increasing the power further and adapting its output for drag use was simply a question of buying the bits and bolting them on. $300 could buy you a 50 per cent increase via a dual-quad carb set-up, a ported, relieved and polished block, Ansen inlet manifold and smart ignition system. Alter the rear-end gear ratios, stiffen-up the rear suspension for good traction and convert the transmission to a slick four-on-the-floor, and you could start dragging without too much danger of severe embarrassment. Gordon Funk was a regular racer at Pomona drags with his year-old '57 Chevy Bel Air. He'd installed a Corvette 283, fitted with a McCulloch blower and a dual-quad system. In '58 the car took 11 wins at 12 meetings, with a best time of 12.27 seconds and 109.54 mph.

In that year the Editor of *Hot Rod* wrote: 'Gone are the days when hot rodders were looked upon as speed-happy maniacs with definitely suicidal tendencies. Today Detroit recognizes the value of the "basic research" performed by these mechanical marvels. There can be no doubt that most of the mechanical improvements of today's cars are due largely to the painstaking work done by eager, oil-smeared rodders in out-of-the-way, barn-to-garage converted workshops.' The racers' effect on the motor manufacturer may not have been quite that considerable, but Detroit was certainly locked into brute power as part of their market-catching strategy — the copyline on the Lincoln ad read: 'The first function of a fine car is outstanding performance'. Pontiac enticed potential customers not only to tune into their *Red Buttons Show* on Fridays on NBC TV, but also to 'Thrill to Strato-Streak V8 performance as exciting as its name!' Chrysler boasted 250 bhp and its PowerFlite automatic transmission — Chevrolet had Turboglide, Glide-Ride and Turbo-Fire — and De Soto offered Firedomes and Fireflites. America was power-conscious, and that did the power-orientated motor sports no harm at all.

Drag racing turned the decade and came hurtling into the Sixties with terminal speeds getting higher and ETs getting lower. The NHRA ban on fuels wasn't lifted until 1963, but did in its way prove helpful; rather than trying to depend on external additives, like exotic fuels, the engine builders had to concentrate on basics. There was a fad for double-engined cars. A flirtation really, (though as late as '72 Freight Train was dominating AA/GD, and in '71 Walt Stevens' Odd Couple slingshot — so named because one mill was a blown and injected Chevy and the rear one was a blown and injected 392 Hemi — took Top Gas at the Winternationals) and having watched a double-engined drag bike develop a fault on one mill, which then went on to tear the second mill apart, I can perhaps see why. Too much hassle and far too expensive without a particularly spectacular result.

1962 saw the first ever sub-8-second pass, with Tommy 'TV' Ivo just

Dave Strickler, seen here leaving the line in an experimental Dodge factory sedan, was one of the entries for the first British International Drag Festival which Sydney Allard worked so hard to promote before he died.

cutting through with a 7.99. In 1966 Don Westerdale recorded a terminal speed of 210.76 mph to break the 200-mph barrier for the first time, and the first man to break into the 6s was Don Prudhomme with a 6.99 ticket in 1967.

Apart from the continuing development of ultra-streamlined bodies and various experiments with chassis lengths and styles, there were two major advances in that decade. Firstly, the driver's position shifted. Tony Nancy was the first 'modern' racer to build a front-seat fueller — The Wedge. His was not the first front-seat Dragster, by a long way, but Nancy was the first guy to redesign the current fueller style to place the cockpit ahead of the engine (it's slightly misleading to hear them described as 'rear-engined' as the engine position was hardly moved; it was the driver's position that shifted). This layout not only provided a better frontal elevation — the cockpit screen offered a smoother 'face' than the slab front of a blown mill, but also allowed the rear axle to be narrowed further so that the whole profile of the car could be squeezed in still more as the track was reduced. Nor were the drivers sorry to see the potentially explosive clutch relocated from between their legs!

The second major change of the Sixties concerned the available engines. Hemis. Until the aluminium engine arrived, the first of which was Ed Donovan's 417, the racers' choice was the so-called 'Iron Motor' — a strengthened and water channel-less variation on the 392 Hemi. The engine builders such as Ed Pink, Keith Black, Milodon and Donovan fought it out between themselves. The one outsider which came near to ending the Chrysler-derived Hemi's supremacy was the SOHC mill brought out and heavily backed by Ford in the late-Sixties.

It wasn't until 1951 that Chrysler produced their first V8 engine, but that was a 331 Hemi, which allowed Chrysler to claim that their produce that year were America's most powerful production cars. In the early-Sixties Chrysler V8s could be found in various European cars such as Jensens, Facel

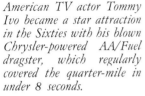

American TV actor Tommy Ivo became a star attraction in the Sixties with his blown Chrysler-powered AA/Fuel dragster, which regularly covered the quarter-mile in under 8 seconds.

Vegas and Bristols, and then, in 1966, they came in on the crest of the latest street-muscle wave. First in their Plymouth firecrackers, then in the big Dodge killers, Chrysler let slip the staggering 426 Hemi. The engine had been around in factory race cars for a couple of years, but now you could drive out of a showroom with 425 bhp and 490 lb ft torque at 4,000 revs under the hood. The racers caught on quick, and haven't let go.

Towards the end of the Sixties and on into the Seventies, low times — 6s and even the first 5 (5.974 by the late Mike Snively on a *losing* run in 1972) — became not only the rule, but within the reach of an increasingly large number of racers. Aerofoils of varying sizes and designs ebbed and flowed with fashion, two-speed shifters and specialist clutches got the power through with increasing speed and efficiency, slick tyre manufacturers came up with new compounds — even stickier, and chassis builders moved into high technology and stress equations. By the mid-Seventies, trying to keep that edge, chassis builders were even installing offset front wheels to keep the car in stage to try and gain vital hundredths of a second.

The late-Sixties and early-Seventies saw the rise of the Funny Car class — an attempt to form a bridge between the top ranks of what we would call Comp Altereds and Top Fuellers. As the fuellers went up into the technological stratosphere, the Funny Car, with its replica production-car body (albeit very heavily modified) forged a link of identity with the spectators — it was really a thin-walled glass-fibre body dropped over a close relative of a Dragster, but it did look like a radically customized Mustang II/Vega/Camaro, or whatever. Now, closely followed by the Pro Stockers (which are restricted under NHRA rules to American engines in American bodies), Funny Car is just about *the* most popular and hotly contested top class, and one which has created considerable feedback to the stylists' drawingboards in Detroit.

In many ways the roots of the Funny Car were entwined around the furious works teams of the early-Sixties. In 1964 Jack Chrisman was campaigning a factory-owned Mercury Comet which, with injected methanol, was turning in timeslips of mid-9s/140 mph. Ramchargers was the name of the Dodge dealer team with covert factory backing — using drag racing as a test bed for new engines in much the same way that they used NASCAR racing — and indeed that was where the 426 Hemi first appeared in drag competition. The first definitive Funny Car is generally reckoned to have been Dyno Don Nicholson's flip-topped, tube-chassised glass-fibre-bodied Ford SOHC-powered Mercury Comet of '66. The glass-fibre was the first alternative to acid-dipped steel; then came staggeringly expensive aluminium replica bodies! These cars qualified for a complete class of their own — Factory Experimental (A/FX) — and were running shell bodies over hell-for-leather racers. By '68 they were using fuel blowers, and were starting to experiment with their now-established glass-fibre replica bodies. While the street muscle war raged, there was a lot of prestige to be gained — what a magical promotional exercise, to have what *appears to be* your latest ultra-butch hunky-coupe running 9s, 8s, or whatever, on a drag strip! At the end of the decade these A/FX machines were starting to look like contemporary Funny Cars and by '73, with Funny Car pioneers such as Gene Snow, the new class had become firmly established.

With nitro-burning engines pumping out more than 2,000 bhp, and times being computed with greater accuracy as top fuellers nudge down to 5.5 seconds for the standing quarter-mile, (at the time of writing Don Garlits holds the world record with his 5.63/250 hit in Ontario in '75) it can seem as if drag racing has reached its horizon. Surely there is a cut-off point, a final time, beyond which a piston-driven car simply cannot go?

Ah, *piston-driven;* the pit-pundit treats you to a knowing wink and confides the great secret. The drag car of the future, he assures you, will hurtle to incredible times under jet or rocket propulsion. The cars, in admittedly small numbers, already exist; rocket drag cars run low-4s. Low-4s! Surely, then, there is another cut-off point looming — the speed of mere human reaction, the ability to aim true and survive the G-forces? On the other hand, those wild young bucks who urged their flathead roadsters along the concrete of the Orange County Airport in the high summer of 1950 would never have believed a street-legal road car running 9s, or a rail cutting high-5s, let alone . . . no, they'd have laughed at you and drenched you with beer from a half-opened much-shaken bottle of Budweiser . . . let alone a low-4.

Thirty years on and into their middle age, any one of those guys must look at modern strips, cast his mind back to the pioneer summers and wonder just what they helped to start. Modern American strips accommodate tens of thousands of spectators (in grandstands too, not on bulldozed earth banking any more), cater for hundreds of racers at every meeting and are large commercial concerns — with all the drawbacks and advantages which that involves. The greatest difference, though, must be the racers themselves — the Funny Car and Top Fuel pilots especially — sponsored up to the eyeballs, their names registered as trademarks and incorporated businesses, negotiating staggering appearance fees and employing full-time highly-qualified crews, publicity conscious and always eager to create an image or a nickname or a reputation for themselves, something that the public and the promoters and the press and the sponsors can latch on to, just as in any major modern sport, be it boxing, tennis, basketball, soccer . . . or drag racing.

All that, though, that's just the wrapping, the packaging which makes the sport available to so many more people. Take it away and leave the 1950 drag-racing hero and the 1982 drag-racing hero together in the pits with a socket set and a misfiring motor and they'd be back to basics within seconds. They'd be talking the same language, working with the same speed and inherent expertise, filling in the punchlines to each other's jokes and — the mill now firing sweetly and true — they would feel the same timeless excitement as they rolled the car down towards the staging lanes, eager to hurtle themselves towards the horizon — the looney, straightline, fire-powered duellists.

Coming Together

THE BRITISH CLUBS

British Drag Racing Association

The landmarks in British drag racing are numerous and the achievements awe-inspiring. There have been many names — some now forgotten, some newer yet equally distinguished, and some simply shining down through the years like a reassuring win light. These guys have approached so many seemingly impassable barriers and driven through; it's a long-way indeed from 10s to 5s. The one watershed year in British dragging, though — the year which saw the sport with its first truly permanent venue (and so many other firsts) — must be 1967.

Santa Pod Raceway had opened for business the previous year, but the '67 season was when it really found its feet. The strip was a much sparser place than the Pod we know today. Endless white-painted crash barriers, a PA system, a christmas tree which was occasionaly augmented by a marshal with a flag, a black-and-white chequered timing booth and the lonely control tower; add several dozen enthusiastic and dedicated racers, the promotion and club support necessary to get the whole thing going and a very fair-sized crowd and there's Santa Pod of '67.

There would be names you'd still recognize from that season of so many years ago — and cars, too. Nobby Hills was already on to his third Houndog. The first Stagecoach was running healthy 13s. Allan Herridge's Cadillac-engined Motovation rail held the B/D class record at 10.68. Geoff Jago took one of his early T-buckets to a 14-second best in Street Altered, while in the same class Clive Skilton was only managing 17s in his Opus-bodied T — though he spent a very successful season racing both the T and his 427 Stingray street motor. Dave Riswick — a USAAF serviceman then and boss of John Woolfe Racing now — drove Mark Stratton's Hustler Comp Altered to a mid-12. Allan Allard's blown 1,650-cc Anglia was running 13s in Comp Altered with a 200-bhp rating. The late John Woolfe dragged his big-milled Shelby Cobra street car; Gerry Cookson was running Trouble Shooter; and Dennis Priddle was running 12s in Tony Gane's Wicked Lady rail.

That season saw the first ever Ladies' Eliminator at the Annual Championship; Christine Skilton, Clive's wife, raced her E-type convertible and was able to add a trophy of her own to those of her husband.

At the June meeting the 91 native racers were met by The American Commando Drag Race Team, fielding furious street cars and a brace of dragsters. Their fuel-injected twin-Buick-powered rail covered the quarter in 9 and looked truly outrageous, but it was bettered by Bud Barnes' Ultrasonic rail and its 8.47/189 time slips. That same meeting ran on into the dark with Britain's first ever night . . . well, dusk meeting. The RAC specified that the eliminations had to be over before lighting-up at 10 pm. For an hour after that, though, they ran match races under floodlights.

1967 also saw the first motorcycle drag championship. The promoters had rashly offered the sum of . . . hmmm . . . £10 for every single-figure two-

Tony Densham was a leading early light of the BDR&HRA and ran The Commuter in the early-Seventies.

The mid-Seventies brought a real coming of age for SPR with the first visit by 'Big Daddy' Don Garlits, just about the greatest name in the American dragging scene.

wheeled pass. Alf Hagon raced his JAP-engined special, with its distinctive Perspex-panelled cone fairing, and not only dominated the finals, but ran a pair of 9s to relieve the promoters of £20.

The organizing club at this time was the British Hot Rod Association, with a membership nearing 1,500. The BHRA had its own magazine — *Drag Racing and Hot Rod* — a surprisingly good read in its time and a history text book today; leaving aside the woman's page ('Rave On'), with its recipes and mascara-applying features, the magazine's contributors included many names and faces — all so youthful then — which remain well-known today and in a couple of cases are now working on the national specialist glossies.

The subject which increasingly crept into the mag's pages towards the end of 1967 was the state of the then-ailing British Drag Racing Association, and there was a public debate about the merits of a merger. Opinions flowed, but the unity factor had it sewn up and 1968 saw British drag racing endowed with not only an increasingly impressive permanent venue, but also a new and larger national club; the British Drag Racing and Hot Rod Association (the BDR&HRA) was with us.

The enthusiastic roots of British dragging stretch back to the late-Fifties, but the first milestone was reached when the decade was only a few years old. A broad spread of hot rodding and dragging fans — mostly already organized in small quasi-American local car park-based clubs, the majority coming from South London — came together following the publication of a unity appeal in *Car Mechanics* magazine, long before a specialist press had been developed. The result, on September 1, 1960, was the founding of the

Headed by Nobby Hills and Owen Hayward, the Houndog team have been to the forefront of British dragging for well over a decade.

British Hot Rod Association.

The infant club looked heavily to the States for its inspiration, and cautious first moves were made to bring organized drag racing to Britain. The club's outlook, though, was far from exclusive to dragging, and perhaps the criticism can be made that their net was spread too wide.

Sydney Allard, performance parts purveyor, expert at rallying Fords and now intrigued by dragging, was of that opinion. In September 1963 he ran his Chrysler Hemi-engined rail against Americans Dean Moon and Mickey Thompson at the Brighton Speed Trials (with Thompson running an 8.84/178). Backed up on the bike side by George Brown, and from across the Atlantic by the legendary NHRA President, Wally Parks, Allard formed the British Drag Racing Association and started planning a season for the following year.

With competitors such as Bootsie Herridge, Bob Phelps, Tony Densham and John Hume, who brought out the Allard kit rail for the first time and piloted it to high 11s, the BHRA, in conjunction with the National Sprint Association, kicked off the '64 season with a meet at Duxford in May. It is said that it was at this meeting that the electronic christmas tree with which we are now so familiar was used for the first time.

The BDRA followed the BHRA with meets at Gravely in June and August, then set about their International Drag Festival — the events known to misty-eyed nostalgic fans as the DragFests.

Thanks to the contacts with the NHRA, a considerable American contingent was persuaded to come over for the six-meeting series. The team included two bikes, two A/FX cars — one of them Ronnie Sox's Mercury — a couple of Willys coupes and a handful of Dragsters, which included two AA-Fuellers — with Tommy 'TV' Ivo and the man who had long since established himself as the Big Daddy of drag racing, the most prestigious driver on Stateside strips, Don Garlits.

With crowds topping out at more than 20,000, times of low-8s and just-sub-200 mph terminals from the big fuellers, and a not inconsiderable purse of prize money and sponsorship, the first DragFest was a great success.

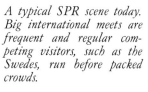

A typical SPR scene today. Big international meets are frequent and regular competing visitors, such as the Swedes, run before packed crowds.

With innumerable new native cars, the second DragFest was being organized for '65 — to take place at Blackbushe and Woodvale in the September and October — with no less than eight AA-Fuellers from the States and a prize purse (according to Mike Lintern's definitive records and memory) of £2,500; meanwhile, the BHRA's big event of the year drew only 500 people to Duxford. Blackbushe has always been known for its tendency

to pull down the clouds, though — a reputation it lived up to that year. Woodvale, near Southport, was a far greater success; so much so that visiting American Buddy Cortines in Troublemaker not only pulled out an all-time fastest British ET of 7.74, but topped the 200-mph terminal mark, too.

It was later that year, as the BDRA was meeting for its AGM, that John Bennett — who had followed founding officer Brian Coole as Chairman — announced that a promotional arm of the club had acquired the use of the old Podington airfield, between Bedford and Northampton, and that they were looking to this site — renamed Santa Pod Raceway — to become Britain's first permanent strip.

Despite running all of 12 meets at the new strip, the '66 season was something of a shakedown year for the raceway. It was, however, a catalystic year. Nothing aids the morale and fortunes of a drag club so much as a permanent strip which they can call their own. Club membership increased, along with member interest in general, and new cars started appearing as if from a production line. Easter at SPR in '67 saw an entry of 70 competitors and a crowd of more than 6,000, which is where we came in.

SPR, now, is Europe's foremost drag strip; the longest established, the best attended and by far the best known. Under the guidance of Bob and Roy Phelps, its name has become synonymous with the sport and it has attracted the greatest American drag racing stars — as well as the impressive block of native drivers who have given so much pleasure to so many spectators over the last decade-and-a-half. Sadly, there isn't space in this brief sketch to give credit to everyone and their achievements . . . where is mention of the organizational talents of Peter and Erica Bartlett? Of the repeated visits by Don Prudhomme and Don Garlits? Or of the Fibre Glass Repairs' creations such as the 427 Stingray wheelie car and the amazing Meglemania Chevy Altered? Of the drag and customs shows organized by the BDR&HRA at the Fairfield Halls, in Croydon, and at the Stratford Drill Hall, in Manchester? Of the Tony Densham Commuter rail, Clive Skilton's Revolution, Walt Ithell's twin-engined Aggravation II, of the FoMoCo/FGR Gloworm Capri — Britains first true Funny Car?

Santa Pod and the BDR&HRA are synonymous; their progress and destinies have been intertwined. To know it you have to be there to see it for yourself, to hear it and to smell it. SPR is top of the pile for rolling thunder in Britain; the loos never seem to get much better, but the racing always does. Also, if you have difficulty in getting your tongue round the initials BDR&HRA, despair no more; towards the end of 1981 the club decided to shorten its name to the more manageable British Drag Racing Association, thereby reviving the initials BDRA.

National Drag Racing Club

The focal point of any drag racing club is, of course, its strip. A club without a strip is like a Toad of Toad Hall sitting in the middle of the road going 'Poop poop'; the club members can only bench race in amenable hostelries over foaming jugs of ale. All very well, but hardly as good as the real thing. For more than a decade the NDRC ran very competent meetings at venues such as Blackbushe and came very close to establishing a full-time strip of their own at Radlett, in Hertfordshire, but never reached real permanence. The corner was finally turned, though, on May 10, 1980.

After months of work — and indeed, with teams of welders still installing the Armco barriers, which had been delivered late because of a long-running industrial dispute — the NDRC unveiled Long Marston raceway, in Warwickshire.

The workmen, the club members and its various officials were still beavering away at noon on that pleasant summer's day. They were within an hour or so of completion — the pits were already filling and the spectator areas were far from empty — but the local ATV television crew needed to have a run in the can for transmission later that day. Hence, prior to the official opening ceremony, Russ Carpenter donned his fire suit and climbed

Keith Harvie, of Americar, in Southend, burns out at an NDRC meet at Silverstone circuit in the early days of the club.

into Glacier Grenade. The welders were pulled back for a moment. The PA crackled into life and Baz Barron launched into a convincing spiel and, untimed, Russ made the first run down the Long Marston quarter. The NDRC were back in business.

At the time of writing the club has just seen the last of its season of eight Long Marston meetings for '81. The set-up down there at Long Marston is a joy; approached directly from a major road — thus obviating the need for a lengthy drive down winding country lanes — and set in beautiful Cotswold countryside six miles south of Stratford-on-Avon. the strip itself is virtually flat and well finished, while the pits and amenities are well laid out and work efficiently. Well supported by solidly loyal local club members and many racers from other areas, the club only has to promote the venue and establish a good and regular gate to make Long Marston one of Europe's top strips.

A year or so after the formation of the BDR&HRA, a group of racers and marshals started to worry about the direction which the club seemed to be taking at that time. Moves were careful and far from divisive; they wanted better marshalling facilities, more democracy — in that they considered that the association's officers held their posts for too long — greater clarity of the financial side of things, and they considered the sport's PR to be inadequate. To give themselves a voice they created a unit within the BDR&HRA and called it the Drag Control and Timing Association, a move which followed a meeting of 50 or so dissenters at Jones Paper Mill, in St Neots — the first of a number of historic meetings held in the oddest places.

At this time the BDR&HRA were holding 'Club' meets, at which the winners received trophies, and 'All Star' meets, where the winners received prize money. At the latter, officials and marshals were paid a fee (varying between £3 and £6) and the DC&TA members put half of their fees into a fund under this separate DC&TA banner — with the simple original intent of buying a Gestetner, to run off pairing notices, and a track van. Meanwhile, they had made a tentative approach to the RAC, asking if they

could gain racing recognition should they ever consider that necessary. The RAC said yes, but that the proposed name was too precise and would have to be changed.

Local DC&TA members met in Huntingdon, Stevenage and the Midlands to discuss their grievances and put on a united front for the BDR&HRA's annual general meeting for 1969, which was held at the Randolph Hotel, in Oxford, early in the October. Little was resolved and the DC&TA met again — in a gym hall — to discuss the situation further. They decided that nothing had been changed to accommodate their ideas, so October 24, 1969 went down as the day that the National Drag Racing Club was formed, still, though, within the BDR&HRA — but with the option of moving out on their own if this manoeuvre still provoked no positive reaction. The split was inevitable, and early in 1970 more than 100 NDRC members braved heavy snows and an influenza epidemic to attend a meeting at the Matrix

The NDRC ran events at Snetterton during the Seventies, with stars like Roz Prior, but eventually the remoteness of the circuit from so many potential spectators made the venue uneconomic.

Mid-morning on May 10, 1980, at the refurbished Long Marston strip where, with the first spectators already in the stands, club officials finish off months of work.

works, in Coventry. The mandate was adopted and the National Drag Racing Club became an independent organization.

The infant club was not destined to have an easy birth, nor indeed a particularly easy childhood. The first crisis occurred when the RAC, as the governing body of all British motor sport, announced that they were no longer allowing the words National or British in club titles. The news arrived just after the NDRC had taken delivery of all its headed notepaper and signs and were committed to bills of around £200. Chairman Alan Wigmore — who, with Tony Weston, had been campaigning the Itzaviva car before becoming involved in the politics and the administration — well remembers a panic phone call which found him as he was visiting a factory in North Wales. (The original committee included Byron Tonge, who was the Secretary, Steve Perry and Cliff Jones, who was eventually to take over from Horace Jakes as the club's Treasurer.)

The club went cap in hand to the RAC, argued their case and finally won a dispensation — but with the condition that the NDRC live up to its title and be a truly national club and run meetings at as many different venues around the country as possible.

In that first year the club organized meetings at Santa Pod on a couple of occasions and ran at Blackbushe in conjunction with Bob Phelps and the SPR crew. Their first independent meeting was a memorable weekend of glorious sunshine and splendid racing at Martlesham Heath, near Ipswich. The Saturday started with two local bobbies in attendance, and the Sunday ended with just about every mobile Suffolk police unit called out to marshal the terrific (and quite unexpected) crowd of 8,000 along the country lanes.

Over the next couple of years the NDRC promoted dragging at Fulbeck, near Newark, in Nottingham; at Dunkefwell, in Devon; at North Luffenham, near Leicester; and at Elvington, up in the North Riding as it was then, where Clive Skilton ran Britain's first native 7 in Revolution 2. Between '73 and '75 the club co-promoted events with Skilton's company, and during that time discovered Wroughton, part of the RAF air museum site, near Swindon, in Wiltshire. In 1976, Super Drags acted as co-promoter, and from '77 onwards the club went out on their own again, running at Snetterton, Blackbushe and Wroughton.

All the while they were on the look-out for a permanent site which they could not only call their own and make into a flagship venue, but which would also help to cut down the costs of erecting and dismantling the racing paraphernalia before and after every meeting. Immense amounts of work have always gone into organizing any drag race meeting, and as inflation increased so dramatically in the late-Seventies, costs inevitably rose enormously.

Snetterton was becoming less of a viable strip as petrol prices rocketed (it was simply situated too far away from the centres of population), Wroughton was an operational RAF site subject to rather different long-term plans, and Blackbushe has always been a working aerodrome and must always be ready for use by air traffic on the Monday morning.

Radlett looked perfect, situated as it was so close to junction 5 on the M1. A lot of work followed demonstration runs for the local council, and two meetings were held there in 1978. The first problem, though, was the weather; '77 and '78 were washout years — one of those things no-one could do anything about. At best they seemed always to have damp tracks and poor times; at worst — as at Wroughton on one occasion — the strip was covered with an inch of water! Then Radlett's local authority revoked the planning permission for the racing, and that ended a couple of pretty unfortunate years for the NDRC.

Long Marston had not been a venue for the club since 1975, though NDRC Midlands (a division of the NDRC according to RAC rules, but in practice an almost autonomous body) had been running eighth-mile dragging there fairly regularly. Realizing the pressing need for a permanent strip — and the need for a boost to the club members' and officials' morale — the national body took a new look at the North Cotswold venue and entered into negotiations with the owners. The basic problems, it seemed,

would be few — all that would be needed was a considerable amount of money and an even greater amount of sheer hard work. By late-'79 an arrangement had been made with the owners, the club members had responded superbly to a fund-raising appeal and work started in earnest the following spring.

As Alan Wigmore said: 'Life has sometimes been difficult for the NDRC', but a fair degree of good luck seemed to be with them at Long Marston, and with the dedication of the club that was (and remains) a formula for success. The new strip is very much on the map and is repaying the club for their effort many times in sheer satisfaction. At the time of writing there is some uncertainty over their future at Blackbushe; as part of a wider plan the area used for racing has been resurfaced and new approach roads have been built. All that is needed is renewed permission from the local council for the Hampshire venue to become a good second string to the NDRC's new-found permanence at Long Marston.

Old meets new. In original condition, with its blown four-cylinder Ford engine, an Allard kit slingshot (which would have cost just £645 in 1968) leaves the line at the new-look Long Marston strip.

Pennine Drag Racing Club

The Sixties were lonely years for the small band of dedicated guys who lived in the so-called north, which in reality starts hardly a third of the way up the mainland of Britain. Santa Pod was the most northerly drag strip, yet it was 150 miles away from places like Leeds, Bradford, Halifax and Huddersfield. Heaven knows how a drag freak would get on in Widdybank Fell, let alone Aberdeen or Tomnavoulin.

Not that the distance was any deterrent to these northerners, though. They did a bit of sprinting — mostly on bikes — on their own account and got together, eight or nine of them, to trek down the newly-opened M1 to the Pod, like motorized Celts lobbying Hadrian's Wall — and they got the same sort of reaction; trouble a't'mill — what sort of a joke's that?

They could ride their bikes, though. Godfrey Wormald was a class champion on his blown 350, running regular 10s. Steve Murty won *his* class championship, too on a blown 1,000-cc Vincent. No messing about. Later on he used to race a 1,200-cc-powered Model Y down at the Pod and held his class record for quite some time . . . with a time of 24 seconds, the only competitor in the class, so he was the slowest, too.

They called themselves the Pennine Drag Racing Team, this minibus load, and during the late-Sixties they earned themselves more than trophies

Clive Skilton's superb Vaux-hall VX 4/90 Funny Car at Aintree where, unfortunately, top cars failed to bring in the paying public in sufficient numbers.

both at the Pod and on the mainland of Europe. The communal dream, though, was their own strip. Aye, all well and good for a handful of mechanics, plus a couple of apprentices and a farmer.

Dave Witham, though, was a flying nut, and he had copies of some old Air Ministry maps pinpointing airfields. It was no hard task to discover which were disused, so the lads went looking. They checked out more than 50, and were just about to embark on the examination of 50 more, when, to their surprise and delight, one came up for sale. It's not often airfields come up for sale, so Dave didn't hang about. He went out and bought it.

Crosland Moor was a desolate site, up on the moors above Huddersfield, and whipped by the relentless Pennine winds. On the plus side, though, it was near the temporary end of the part-finished M62 and was midway between Manchester and Leeds, with both hardly 20 miles away.

Godfrey and Murt formed themselves into Pennine Raceway Limited and set about looking for the finance that would be needed to turn paved heathland into a paying drag strip. All the gang set about boosting the club's membership in the meantime. To be recognized by the RAC the Pennine Drag Racing Club had to have a minimum of 50 members, so many of those new members were girlfriends and parents and mates from work.

The snow-swept month of February 1974 saw work begin. They finished at their jobs 5.30, had their teas, and went up to the Moor to work through the evening. Ne'mind the cold, ne'mind the darkness.

The work was finished by the summer, and in June the club ran the first of its two shakedown meetings while they planned a full calendar for '75. Already the ACU had granted them a round of bike competition for the new season. There were 10,000 spectators up on Crosland Moor for those two meetings, but while those 10,000 folk were delighting in the north's first drag meetings, the local Kirkless Council were receiving complaints by the dozen. Well, one dozen, and on the strength of those 12 complaints they applied directly to the Secretary of State asking for the strip's planning permission to be revoked. It was a unique move for a local council to make with regard to any form of motor sport and, for the handful of upstanding

Dennis Priddle in his 1974 Avenger Funny Car smoking the tyres at a wild and windswept Crosland Moor.

Sitting in stage at Aintree in 1975 is Pat Cuss in the streamlined, fuel-injected Hemi-powered Ratcatcher rail.

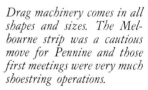

Drag machinery comes in all shapes and sizes. The Melbourne strip was a cautious move for Pennine and those first meetings were very much shoestring operations.

councillors, a successful one. Pennine had their world sliced away from beneath them. The investment of both time and money was destroyed.

With the help of Clive Skilton's European Drag Racing Promotions, Pennine picked itself up and arranged to transfer two of its 1975 meetings to Aintree, in Liverpool. These dates were very well supported by the racers and the field included Dennis Priddle and Clive Skilton in their Funny Cars, and Roz Prior and Trevor Young. The venue was not a financial success, though. As Murt puts it: 'The first Aintree meeting was a disaster . . . and the second was a complete disaster'.

The club was strong enough by then, with 150 (true) members and more than 70 local race cars, but a drag club needs a strip. In Pennine's case the club could not finance its own raceway, only the *entrepreneurs* could do that. If the whole thing had slid quietly away in the autumn of '75 few people would really have been surprised and that would have been that.

1976 came and went. Then, early in '77, the impetus started coming back to the club with the renewed interest in a private airfield amid lush pasture on a large farm near the village of Melbourne, in what is now Humberside.

Raymond Foster, the Club Secretary of the time, had 'discovered' the Melbourne airfield as early as 1974, but inspection had shown that it would have needed a fortune spent on it to transform it into a viable strip. It was obvious now that the fortune was going to have to be spent. Murt formed a partnership with his wife, Leone, called it Pennine Promotions, and set about raising some finance, yet again. Meanwhile, the same crew — those truly dedicated committee members and racers — set-to in work parties, armed with spades and wheelbarrows, clearing the sods and filling the holes, yet again.

June 26, 1977, and a sparse Melbourne strip opened for business. It was a good day, fun. The sun shone and there was real excitement and a wonderful communal thrill. I came back to the next of those two summer-'77 meetings as support for Alastair McFarlane and his Jago Jeep. The Jeep took well to dragging, but still got beaten. Hell, it was a smashing day out, though. Pennine had turned the corner and, slowly and steadily rather than with great bounds, were coming into British drag racing as a viable club and raceway.

With five meetings in each successive year, their September '80 meet was a celebration — The Pennine Drag Racing Club's 21st race day. Seventeen of those had been at Melbourne — renamed The New York Raceway early in '79 — and not one had ever been rained off. Just as they had dedicated themselves to creating and sustaining good relations with the landowner, the local inhabitants, the police and those members (that member) of the specialist press who could be bothered to haul themselves up to a dot on the map *actually north of Goole* from their first meeting on, they've been blessed with the best weather of any British drag racing venue. No, I'm not tempting fate — I've said that in print so many times that I'd have broken the spell years ago were the fates to be tempted.

The facilities at New York Raceway are good. At the end of '80 they built a new startline tower and relegated their old bus to the role of VIP lounge behind the fire-up lane. The club has lost none of its warmth and friendliness, and the promoters haven't tried to over-reach themselves or jeopardize the casual yet competitive feel of their meets. With landmarks such as the Street Racing Championships in '79, '80 and '81 to their credit, and having been the European pioneers of truck dragging, all the New York Raceway needs now is a new quarter-mile of asphalt, and to iron out some of the bumps and potholes in the entrance roads and the return road. Still, all that'll come, doubtless.

Class Distinction

THE RACE CLASSES

Dragster

Everyone's mental image of the classic drag car; the rail. A long narrow chassis supported by tiny motorcycle-like wheels at the front and slicks on huge mag wheels at the back, with a tiny cockpit and a huge engine some place in the middle. Dragsters range from the lean monsters which run constant 6s and the occasional 5, to smaller and older machines with times in double figures.

Engines in Dragster class are quite unrestricted, apart from the general guidelines — which are as for Funny Car (next section). The one thing the rule book does say is that, should you want, you can have two mills rather than one. More the merrier, I suppose. The car's ECW ratio divides the Dragster class into Senior, Middle and Junior.

The ECW is the car's 'effective capacity to weight' ratio, and is determined by relating the dry weight of the car in ready-to-race condition against its engine's capacity (always measured in cubic inches). If a blower is fitted, 40% is added to the capacity; 25% if nitromethane fuel is being used; and 75% for both. In Dragster class there is an additional allowance added to the weight total which assumes 150 lb for the driver.

Senior Dragster divides into three ECWs, all minimums; 3.00 - 3.49 lb/ci for AD, 3.50 - 4.49 lb/ci for BD, and 4.50 - 5.49 lb/ci for CD. Dragsters with side-valve engines have a minimum ECW of 2.50 lb/ci. Middle Dragster ECWs are 5.50 - 6.24 in DD and 6.25 - 6.99 in ED. Junior Dragster ECWs are 7.00 - 7.74 in FD, and anything over 7.75 for GD. All ECWs are common to both the NDRC and the BDRA.

I mentioned blowers and 'fuel' (nitromethane mixture) above, and this is where the Top Fuellers come in. Although there are only a handful in the country at any one time, these are the monsters of drag racing; quite simply, the Dragsters which, belching the heady crackling fumes of nitro, run faster than anyone else. The current piston-driven British drag record for a quarter-mile pass is still the 5.97 put down by Peter Crane at Santa Pod Raceway's Easter meeting in 1975. Top Fuellers have been losing out a touch in the popularity stakes to the Funny Cars, but their numbers are really being depleted by simple economics. Increasingly the big rails compete in Pro Comp (of which more when we get on to Comp Altereds), tending to run blowers with gas rather than fuel. Many people do feel that the day of the Top Fueller is over, and the future lies in Pro Comp, Econo classes and the new Fuel Altered classes, which are unknown over here so far (1981).

When it comes to the construction of the Dragster body, the NDRC decrees: 'The body, wind deflector and cowl must be constructed of metal, fibreglass, or other suitable flameproof material, and must extend forward to the firewall'; which means that there must be a body of some sort separating the cockpit from the engine. This cockpit must be so designed

Jim Read is one of the most respected figures in European drag racing. Le Patron runs a Donovan mill and competes in Pro Comp.

The blown Daimler Hemi of the AE Hepolite-sponsored Glacier Grenade dragster can only lay claim to 2½ litres, but it has proved a strong, reliable and fast motivator for Russ Carpenter.

Ever the showman, Russ Carpenter can boast the come-liest support crew in the business for his Glacier Grenade rail.

A greatly narrowed rear axle on a Top Fuel dragster. Note the disc brakes and the parachute connection on the top of the diff, with its operating cables above.

that no part of the driver's anatomy can come into contact with the wheels, tyres, engine or the track in the event of any kind of crash. There must be a full floor, and there must be a separate floor where the driver's legs are routed under the rear axle.

A Dragster with a wheelbase of more than 180 inches need not have front suspension. Sufficient positive castor must be incorporated in the car's front end to ensure good handling at any speed. Only proven car steering can be used, and that must turn the Dragster round within two parallel lines 15 metres apart.

A Dragster must have at least two independent braking systems and at least two hydraulic rear wheel brakes are essential. The brakes may be operated by hand or foot, and a hand-operated brake lever must be located inside the cockpit. Disc brakes are essential on cars capable of speeds in

The engine on Bob Harman's Lo-Litre DD dragster is a tiny 996-cc Puma Weslake ex-bike parallel-twin. It runs good times, though.

Typical of the many tidy mid-budget and moderately engined dragsters running in Britain is Roy Green's Resurrection rail. Its 3-litre Ford engine has taken it to 12.40/109.

All new for 1982 and the lightest car he reckons he's ever built, Dennis Priddle turned out his latest Top Fuel dragster at the '81 Fireworks meeting at Long Marston.

The bodywork on Priddle's new car has been left in its naked aluminium state – he reckons that he can live without the extra 20 lb which paint would weigh. Early runs proved that more aerofoil-induced downthrust was needed to keep it on the track.

excess of 150 mph. Brake lines must be routed outside chassis or frame rails, and where they pass the flywheel area they must be cased in steel tubing with a minimum wall thickness of ⅛-inch.

Fuel pumps must be electrically operated, but can be of any type. Fuel blocks are permitted, and the regulations demand an ignition switch, which: 'Must be wired to cut off the electrical supply, otherwise a remote-control quick-action shut-off valve, operable by the driver in the normal position, must be located in the main fuel line, between the tank and the carburettor or injector'. As fuel lines pass the bellhousing they must be enclosed in steel tubing of ⅓-inch wall, and this must be securely fixed. The rule book recommends similar protection for fuel lines passing blowers and blower belts.

As far as the electrics go, instruments may be added or subtracted — though in these leagues they tend to be as basic as possible. The battery or batteries (maximum of two and weighing no more than 150 lb) may be located wherever, but it is recommended that they be as far from the fuel supply as possible. Ignition wiring must be routed outside the chassis rails and must go through steel tubing of ⅛-inch wall where it passes the flywheel bellhousing and be securely attached. Most Dragsters have a minimal electrical system and no self-start facilities.

When it comes to the Dragster's transmission, explosion-resistant flywheels and pressure plates are obligatory. A flywheel shield must also be fitted. All cars fitted with automatic transmission must have a protective blanket of at least ¼-inch steel around the box. Any type of transmission may be fitted. A prop catcher must always be fitted, and the rule book 'highly recommends' that a torque tube of at least ⅛-inch thickness be employed to enclose the prop-shaft.

Any type of rear axle may be used. Where the driver sits over or behind the diff, a suitable protection shield should be used to guard against explosion. Safety hubs are recommended. 'All cars using Hotchkiss type of drive-shaft and rear suspension must have radius arms, traction bars, or some suitable pinion support to prevent rear-end housing rotation.' The rear axle can be rigid; and in fact always is.

A proper seat must be made up for the driver, and must be upholstered and adequately mounted — taking into consideration the possibility of a crash. The seat must be supported at the bottom and at the back of the frame or cross-member. There must be satisfactory padding, and a padded headrest to prevent whiplash damage is recommended.

Wheels: Alloy wheels are fine. Wire wheels or motorcycle spoked wheels are allowed on the front — providing the car doesn't weigh more than 1,800 lb. 'Such wheels must be equipped with steel spokes of adequate diameter properly cross-laced to provide the maximum strength.' All spoked wheels must be fully laced; no leaving out spokes to reduce weight.

In the soggy summer of 1980 Russ Carpenter put his Hepolite Glacier Grenade into the 7s with a 7.80 and a 7.92 — and all with a tiny 2½-litre Daimler Hemi engine. Russ is a very successful racer — and a sponsor's delight — and had been campaigning this all-British rail for several years. If ETs were related to engine capacity, Russ and John Whitmore — who built the BL-powered and sponsored Drag N Fly, another highly competitive all-native dragster — would be well ahead of the rest of the world.

Funny Car

Funny Car: Silly expression really. It denotes a dragster of unrestricted size and power which is covered over with a body which is a loose replica of a production car. Funny Cars have only evolved over the last decade and are now just about the most popular top class of drag car.

The NDRC rule book describes Funny Cars as: 'Cars constructed for all-out competition, but fitted with a saloon or coupe body originally produced not more than five years ago, or replica thereof.' The bodies, in fact, are

always replicas, made of thin glass-fibre, totally unadorned, though panelled internally, and hinged from the rear to open up and provide access to both the engine and the cockpit. The production model upon which the replica is based, as they say above, must not be more than five years out of date.

The rules permit radical body modifications, and these are usually taken advantage of. The top of the car may be chopped down by 2 inches and the car's length may be altered by up to 10%. If doors are not functional (and they never are) then the side window areas must be left open and be large enough for the driver to get in and out. Alternatively there must be an escape hatch on the roof. Or, for the claustrophic, both. The means of operating the body's hatch must be clearly marked.

The engine must be completely sealed from the driver by a firewall, but in front of that anything can happen — you can fit any sort of engine you fancy, and it can be supercharged or turbocharged. The mill can be relocated and there are no restrictions on internal modifications. Open exhausts are allowed. Drive belts for superchargers and fuel pumps must have a protective steel plate covering three-quarters of the length and be the same width, the steel to be no less than $\frac{1}{8}$-inch thick. You don't need cooling, unnecessary electrics, or a permanently on-board starter.

The type and construction of the Funny Car's frame or chassis is free from restrictions, but must incorporate a full roll cage conforming to the standards laid down. All butt welds must be visibly reinforced and you can't go grinding welds down too much. A Funny Car's wheelbase must be between 100 and 125 inches. Regulations for the fuel system, parachutes, roll bar spec, brakes, electrics, transmission and upholstery are as for Dragster.

Steel or magnesium car-style front wheels are mandatory, and must be at

Funny cars never fail to excite the crowd at a drag meeting and, like Graham Hawes' Black Magic, they are almost always beautifully turned out.

The Swedes are particularly hot on Funny Cars. This is Lee Anders' Red Barron, with replica Monza body and Milodon mill. Rear tyre sidewall wrinkles are clearly evident.

A rare line-up of Funny Cars was provided when British and Swedish machines were assembled at Santa Pod in the warm summer sun of 1979.

Funny Car bodies must bear some passing resemblance to the original production car and often, as with this Corvette, the end result can actually be an improvement on what the manufacturer intended.

least 14-inches diameter by 4-inches rim width. It is recommended that racing tyres are used on those front wheels (but in practice are usually M & H's semi-slick Front Runners).

Unlike Dragsters, Funny Cars must have front suspension, and it must work. 'Sufficient positive castor must be incorporated in the front end to ensure proper handling of the car at all speeds.' The rear axle can be free of suspension, and always is. The rule book dictates that: 'Only proven automobile steering systems are permitted', so basic rack-and-pinion or recirculating-ball are fine. The Funny Car must be able to turn completely within two parallel lines which are 13.5 metres apart, and why the rule book should go metric on that dimension when everything else is in imperial, I don't know.

The width of the rear tread must be such that the slicks do not protrude outside the body line, nor are more than 3 inches inside it. Front tread widths must be such that the tyres are no more than 6 inches inside the body; measurements are all taken from the outside of the tyre to the inside of the body. Butterfly steering wheels are permitted.

Dennis Priddle is one of the most respected drivers in European dragging. His soft accent, which gives away his origins in England's West Country, has been heard in drag strip pits for many years. Sponsored by the performance people John Woolfe Racing, Dennis campaigned both a

Funny Car and a rail for some time, using a single interchangeable power plant and transmission unit.

The Funny Car's body was based on a Chevrolet Monza, and it was an impressively smart car. The engine was a heavily worked Chrysler 426 Hemi and the blower a Littlefield 6:71 fitted with Enderle fuel injection. The transmission was a Lenco two-speed (plus reverse), and the power came through a Crowerglide triple-plate clutch.

The car was four years old in 1981, though it had been modified and improved in that time. A new and lower frame was built for it in '78 and the body reworked — and brought down in overall height by 4 inches. The engine was stroked to 484 ci, and ran around 82% nitro, with the blower overdriven by between 35% and 45%.

The Monza tended to run very consistent mid-6s, its best time to date being the 6.50 Dennis turned in on his very first outing in the car.

Campaigning a Funny Car is a frighteningly expensive business. An average day's outing can certainly see off a pair of rear slicks, four or five pistons, a handful of valves, and then there's the expense of a complete oil and plug change betweeen every round! It goes without saying that a complete engine and chassis teardown and rebuild between meets takes up more than a little time and, inevitably, a goodly sum in cash.

Dennis Priddle maintains a single chassis and engine and alternates the bodywork to enable him to run the machine as either a Top Fuel dragster or a Funny Car.

Competition Altered

Competition Altered is probably the best-populated series of classes in European dragging. A Comp Altered car is built for all-out competition, but must have a body which was originally manufactured for a road-going car, or is a replica thereof. This very general formula means in practice that the class covers all sorts of machines, from small-engined machines with cut-down car bodies, right up to the 6 and 7-second Pro Comp cars.

Competition Altereds are divided into three classes: Senior, Middle and Junior, by ECW ratios of 3.00, 4.50 and 7.00 lb/ci, respectively. Pro Comp is not a separate class in the rule books, but is a category which brings together Dragsters, Funny Cars and Comp Altereds at the top end of the Comp Altered scale which meet one of three requirements: Supercharged engines running without nitro, cars running with nitro but without superchargers, or supercharged and nitro-powered cars which have a capacity of less than 250 ci. There are also ECW restrictions and in the top class rating cars are limited to a two-speed transmission. Very much an up-and-coming category, Pro Comp brings together so many of drag racing's most exciting elements and such a large number of divergent cars that it is

Campaigned by the Page family, Panic is one of Europe's best known and most successful Comp Altereds. Years of experience show in both the preparation and the driving.

Dave Hurt calls it The Animal. A Funny Car-style hinged Hillman Imp body is raised above a 331-ci Chrysler mill, but when lowered it gives the car a distinctive nose-diving stance.

Suspension is mandatory on Comp Altereds, but it is hardly up to road-going specification. This set-up on a drop-tube axle is about as sophisticated as it gets.

usually *the* most popular event in the programme of a class meeting . . . and by and large, when the Pro Comp chips are down, it's a bitch trying to get round the heavy Swedes.

Some Comp Altereds run stock Pop bodies and the like, some have standard steel or glass-fibre car bodies which have been lightened and cut 'n shut, while others, Funny Car-like, have flimsy glass-fibre replica bodies. Extensive customizing is allowed, so long as the basic car is still recognizable. The body can be chopped, channelled, or sectioned, but by no more than 10 inches. Comp Altereds are all-out competition cars.

The car's body must not be set back more than 20 inches from standard, the distance measured from the rear axle to the centre of the original rear wheelarch. When the driver is sitting in the car with his crash helmet on, the roof must be no less than 3 inches above him. As on Funny Cars, if the doors do not open then the window area must be left unglazed, or an escape hatch can be fitted in the roof. Where glass is used it must be safety glass. If side windows are fitted then they must be at least 40 centimetres wide by 25 centimetres high. Doors must be fitted with mechanical (not electrical) handles, inside and out. The engine must be totally sealed from the cockpit by a firewall.

The Hazletons' Thunderbird, which made a great impression on drag meeting crowds in both Britain and on the Continent.

Jean Tidswell comes from Shipley, in West Yorkshire, and must be chasing Sylvia Hauser for the title of Best Publicized Queen of Drag Racing. Her slick Model T was due to have a replacement body.

The regulations concerning braking, transmissions, upholstery, fuel systems and electrical systems are as for Dragster. All classes are obliged to be fitted with parachutes where only one method of braking is fitted, or where the class terminal speed record is over 150 mph. Parachutes must be from a recognized manufacturer, must be independently mounted, and must not be attached to the same bracket as the seat belt — else in the event of a mounting failure when the 'chute opens, the driver could be dragged out of the car by the parachute, leaving the machine to trundle on its way.

Any make or model of car engine can be fitted to a Comp Altered. The engine can be moved from its stock position, but cannot be set further back by more than 30%, this being measured from the centre of the front wheel spindles to the nearest spark plug. Rear-engined cars are allowed if both engine and body came originally from a rear-engined production car. Blower drive belts must be fitted with a shield, as on Funny Cars. Open exhausts are permitted.

The car's frame or chassis may be original specification, or may be altered at the builder's discretion; alternatively, it may be of one-off tubular framing. All butt-welds must be reinforced and welds must not be excessively ground. All cars must be fitted with a regulation-dimension roll-cage, and the Comp Altered's minimum wheelbase is 72 inches.

All Comp Altered race cars must have working front suspension. Sufficient positive castor must be incorporated at the front to ensure good handling. Rear axles may be rigidly mounted without suspension. Proven car steering systems only are allowed and a Comp Altered must be able to turn completely within two parallel lines 13.5 metres apart. Mag wheels front and rear are fine with a minimum diameter of 10 inches. Spoked alloy wheels can be used at the front so long as the minimum tyre section measures 2.5 inches. Wire-spoked wheels are not allowed.

Reg Hazelton campaigned Thunderbird with the help of his two sons, John and Brian. With record-breaking terminal speeds in excess of 200 mph to its credit, the car ran in Pro Comp. The engine was a 393 Chrysler Hemi with a 6:71 Littlefield blower and Hilborn fuel injection.

Jean and Stephan Tidswell first brought out Jeans T to run in Comp Altered for the 1980 season. The engine is from their old Jeans E Pop and the turtle-backed T body came from the Hang 'Em High drag team. Piloted by Jean and propelled for 1981 by a 350 Chevrolet, the T has established itself as a 9-second car. Both the Hazeltons and the Tidswells are slick family teams, largely unsponsored, and very popular with crowds everywhere.

Modified

Modified division forms a bridge between Street and Comp Altered. Cars in that class are certainly all-out competition vehicles, but they must retain their identifiable road-going appearance. Any type of saloon car, coupe, roadster, sports car, pickup, or light van can be presented in Modified.

The car's body must be a manufacturer's item, or be a replica of one. The roof line must be at least 3 inches above the driver's head when he is seated in the car wearing his crash helmet. All closed cars must have working doors on both sides of the car and mechanical door handles must be fitted inside and out. The engine must be completely sealed from the car's interior by a firewall. Windows must be fitted, safety glass being recommended for the screen and Perspex for the side windows. As far as mudguards go, all cars must be road legal.

Engines in Modified are free of restriction, so long as you've only got the one. Any internal modification is allowed and inlet and exhaust manifolds are free of restrictions. If a fan is fitted, it must have an adequate guard. The rule book recommends that metal flash-plates be placed over open carbs. The engine may not be relocated, though.

The frame or chassis can be a stock manufacturer's item, can be modified

First seen in its new paint trim at the 1981 Custom Car Show, Sylvia Hauser's Dodge Challenger is setting the pace for an up-turn in the fortunes of Modified.

The Red Devil Camaro is a typical Modified car – big butch muscle taken a step beyond Production and providing very exciting racing with a large degree of street identity.

if you wish, or can be a one-off tubular-constructon frame. As ever, all butt-welds must have visible reinforcement, and excessive grinding of welds is not allowed. The minimum wheelbase for Modified is 72 inches. There are no restrictions on track dimensions.

Brakes must be 'proven automobile equipment' and must operate on all four wheels. Power-assisted braking is okay and all brake lines must be routed outside the chassis or frame rails, or enclosed in steel tubing with a minimum wall of ⅛-inch where they pass the bellhousing. Regulations concerning the electrical and fuel systems are as for Dragster.

Jimmy Briggs took his Wild-man tag with him when he shifted from a Mustang to this 'Woody'-built Ford Maverick, which runs in C/Modified with a 351-ci Cleveland motor.

45

Steve Clifton's C-cab is a unique beast, which was originally built for street use, but when Type Approval regulations loomed the emphasis was shifted to the drags.

The Hot Tomato runs a well set up and highly efficient Rover 3½-litre V8 with a Wade RO34 blower mounted between the mill and the Holley carb.

46

The fitting of street equipment such as numberplates, generator, windscreen wipers, wiper motors, washers, fan and fan belt and horn is optional. Cars must be fitted with at least two 4-inch diameter headlight units, mounted in the original position. Where a car had concealed headlights in stock form, daylight appearance must be maintained. At least two 2-inch diameter rearlights, fitted with car-type lenses, are obligatory. None of these lights need work, but it is recommended that stoplights are functional.

Steering modifications which improve the roadholding are allowed, but only accepted car steering systems can be used. All the usual stuff about front-end positive castor applies, and the turning circle for Modified is 13.5 metres.

The rule book demands explosion-resistant flywheels and pressure plates for cars running in Modified. A flywheel shield must be fitted to all cars, except rear or mid-engined machines, or those of under 2.5 litres engine capacity which are already fitted with a proprietory steel flywheel and an explosion-proof clutch assembly. Any type or make of gearbox, drive-shaft and rear axle may be fitted and all cars must be fitted with a prop-catcher.

Looking good and going like the real thing, Mike Cheley's 383 Chrysler-powered Modified typifies just the way the Yanks do it all.

John Mills' Roadrunner, which ran in Street, Production and even Comp Altered classes before finding its true home in Modified.

The book now insists on a ¼-inch minimum thickness steel shield or a scatter shield for automatic boxes.

All cars in Modified must be fully trimmed throughout, but sound-proofing may be removed. Saloon cars must have four seats and any other vehicle must have at least two. Wheels and tyres are free of restriction, though front tyres must have a street-pattern tread and be at least 4 inches wide.

Modified is a somewhat under-populated class, but from the look of things is on the way up. The Clifton brothers run their cherry-red C-cab at NDRC meetings. This fad street rod style of car is very rare on European strips; with its large flat frontage the car isn't wonderfully aerodynamic — though its blown 3½-litre Rover V8 does haul the C-cab along quite respectably in the 12s.

John Mills' thunderous Plymouth Roadrunner has been seen on British drag strips many times over the years. John bought the car in '79 and really only started his dragging career the following season. Running in Modified he made it to every meeting that year and took the beast to impressive times in the 11s. The Roadrunner was still powered by its original 383, but a new 440 was installed during the '80/'81 winter.

For eliminations at race meetings, Modifed machinery sub-divides into ECW divisions, the pertinent ratios running from 5.50 lb/ci to 17.50 lb/ci to denote A/M at the top and Q/M at the bottom.

Production

Just about every car you passed on your way to work today could probably have qualified as a Production drag car. My Jaguar street car would make the grade — but then so would my wife's Capri.

Production is the base line in drag classes. Any factory-produced car, pickup, or small van which has been homologated as either a car, sports car, or any other vehicle 'regarded as acceptable by the Competition Committee' is okay. Cars must be street legal overall.

The car must retain the original body as it left the factory gates. Moderate customizing is permissible so long as it does not affect the height, length, width, or contour; so chopping, sectioning, or channelling are out. Flares and modest spoilers are fine and you can use glass-fibre items to replace the bonnet and bootlid — though any modification in either area requires additional catches. All doors must open fully as stock and must be fitted with handles both inside and out. The firewall must not be altered or relocated.

The key to Production class lies in what the rule books say about the engine. The only motors allowed are those which were factory options for that particular model in the specific year of manufacture. So if you own a 1300 Capri you can fit anything up to a 3-litre V6. You could take a post-1976 Escort up to RS2000 specification. You cannot go installing V8s, though, and to get real power out of American machinery in Production you will obviously have to steer away from cars of (say) the Fifties and big heavy sedans; late-model muscle machinery which was offered from the showroom with the option of Hemis, 440s, or whatever would be a much better bet.

The engine must have all its accessories still attached and internal modifications are restricted to engine balancing, head porting and polishing. Over-boring to 0.060 in is permitted. Headers and exhaust systems are free, though gases must be carried clear of the car's body. Carburettors can be changed at will, but the stock intake manifold must not be replaced. Air filters can go the way of the carbs, but if you plan to run without one then a metal shield is required as protection against flashback.

The standard electrical system must be kept intact, though electrical accessories may be added. The battery must be safely located in its original position and be of recommended weight and size.

Steering and braking systems must be standard. Pattern manufacture drum shoes, disc pads and calipers are allowed, as are power assistance on both steering and brakes. Suspension may only be altered if the modification can be said to have improved roadholding and handling.

Fuel tanks must be factory equipment in their original location; fuel pumps are free of restrictions, though. As with Street, roll-bars must be fitted to open cars. The vehicles' chassis, unsurprisingly, must be unaltered.

Gearboxes and their housings must be original equipment, but ratios can be changed as long as everything fits inside the box. Shift linkages may be changed without restriction. The final-drive ratios can be altered to any available from the manufacturer's range, but must go inside the stock diff cover. You are not allowed to shave flywheels. Heavy-duty explosion-resistant pressure plates and flywheels are recommended, as are flywheel shields and engine braces.

Virtually any road wheels — stock, widened, or alloy — are allowed in Production, so long as they do not protrude beyond the original body line and wheel diameter and width may be altered. Tyres are as for Street; racing,

The Magician is Ron Pudney Jnr's Mercury Cougar Production racer. The car looks great on the strip......

.....as it does in the pits. The engine bay is particularly well sorted, and this is a very clean car all round.

approved street, or slicks.

To run in Production, a car's interior must have full upholstery and trim panels. Custom trim panels may be used, but a full set of seats must be present and correct, though the front seats may be replaced by lightweight ones so long as they are correctly upholstered.

Although weight breaks differ, in many ways the American equivalent of Production's style is Stock, while their parallel to Street style is Super Stock; in both cases they divide the classes into two, for automatic transmission and manual shifting. The American national record for a Stock eliminator, by the way, is 10.82 seconds at 125 mph at the time of writing, while the best ever race time for Super Stock stands at 9.70 at 139.75. Gulp.

Ron Pudney campaigns his Magician Mercury Cougar in Production class. This model of car seems to be unique in Britain's drag scene and Ron has further distinguished it with a superb paint job. Powered by a 302 breathing a double-pump 650-cfm Holley carb, the Cougar is sponsored by a discoteque and a local Ford main dealer. It runs consistent 14s.

Street/Roadster

When it comes to Street class drag race cars chances are you've got one parked in your drive. So has your dad, and probably your Auntie Emily as well. A Street class car is one which is completely street legal and can meet the basic RAC scrutineering safety regulations (which should be very little problem for an MoT-worthy street car; securing tipping seats, indicating a kill switch adequately and basic fire precautions are all that should concern you). The NDRC specify Street class thus:

'Saloon cars, sports cars, light vans, etc, which may or may not be modified from the original. The only requirement for this division is that the cars must have a current road fund licence, insurance and MoT certificate (if appropriate). Documentary proof of these must be produced for scrutineering.'

The BDRA class of Roadster (designated S for race numbers) corresponds to the NDRC's Street class. Roadster is run on a handicap system, but their Street bracket is an alternative system and brings together

Jack Fletcher's heavy Goat is a typical Street car, an example of pure Detroit muscle for the street and Street, as it were.

1980 NDRC champion Dave Mingay deserted his Goat for this Corvette in 1981 and is seen here in the finals of the '81 Street Racing Championship.

Modified, Production and Roadster without handicaps.

Cars running in Street class are allowed to run on racing tyres, slicks, or street tyres. You can run in Street with open headers provided you can show the scrutineer the brackets that would normally carry the full silencing system. Catch cans must be fitted to oil breathers.

Open cars must be fitted, understandably, with satisfactory roll-cages.

But for the shark teeth, you might wonder why this bog stock-looking Ventora was producing so much smoke.....

.....until you looked under the hood, that is, and found a nitrous oxide-injected 350-ci small-block Chevy.

Hardly looking like a typical American car, this Pinto of 'Dirty' Des Taylor nevertheless made a considerable impact in Street in 1980.

Where a vehicle has a lightly attached windscreen — as on a roadster or a Model T — you may be required to remove the screen altogether or brace it adequately.

All Street cars must carry a fire extinguisher with a minimum weight of 1 kg. BCF, carbon dioxide and Freon-type extinguishers are recommended rather than dry powder. Tyres must be of RAC-approved manufacture — which means stay away from remoulds. Tinted windows are permitted providing they can be seen through from any angle, so reflective coatings are out. All cars — to quote the NDRC again — 'must have a positive acting external return spring attached directly to each carburettor arm and capable of closing the throttle in the event of failure of the throttle

This 351-ci Windsor engine was a trick installation for the Pinto, the rearward location of the V8 leaving ample room for up-front adjustments.

Off the line at Long Marston, Chris Bond, with the aid of 383-ci Mopar power, just pulls a quickie on Steve Hallam and his 318 Charger. Street V8s are the business.

linkage'. All fuel lines must have adequate and proper clips on joints and flexible pipes — a thing worth taking a peep at; many manufacturers skimp on junctions such as these.

Street cars should have little trouble in the scrutineer's bay, but each car is a new case, and if you are knocked back it will only be because the RAC are concerned with your safety and that of the spectators, marshals and other competitiors.

So, having obtained your competition licence and correctly entered the car in the meeting, there's nothing to stop you tootling over to the strip all ready to race your XJ-S, 3-litre Capri, or Skoda Combi . . . nothing, in the last case, apart from derision. Laying down the law about slow cars in Street is neither fair nor reasonable, but there can be no doubt that some of the 20-second cars I have seen on strips have been nothing more than an irritation to the crowd and an embarrassment to other competitors. There is, of course, an argument that everyone has to start somewhere. Fine. My start was with an old 3-litre Capri in Stock trim, which ran mid-16s, and from a personal angle I would like to say that it is not unreasonable to start at that level. Don't stay there, though; complacency and a lack of regard for the crowd are the two major problems stunting Europeam drag racing.

No matter who is behind the wheel, the Holmes brothers' Ventora always stirs the crowd . . . and no-one who drives this outstanding Street car dares ever to be complacent.

Driven by Bill Sherratt, the Ventora emerged victorious in June 1979 at the first ever Street Racing Championship at Pennine's New York Raceway. Looking virtually stock and running — as the rules of the championship decree — on street tyres, the Ventora ran consistent 12s to beat down heavy opposition from some formidable slices of Detroit muscle. Dave Holmes returned to the championship with the Ventora in 1980 and succeeded in beating Bill in his new car to retake the title.

Bill bought the car from Dave Warne a couple of summers earlier, with its beautifully set-up 350 Chevrolet small-block already installed. A fair amount of work was needed to keep the car running really well, and Bill added nitrous-oxide injection. Being a real Street class drag car, the plain red Ventora has been a common sight on the streets of its native Stockport for several years now; truly street and strip.

Des Taylor, from Wakefield, made quite an impact early on in the 1980 season when he debuted his impressive Ford Pinto. Like the Ventora, the Pinto not only makes it into Street class, but is a fearsome Bracket bomber as well. Powered by a 351 Windsor V8 with a 600 cfm Holley double-pumper carb on an Edelbrock manifold, the torque gets down through a C4 automatic box fitted with a B&M Super Holeshot Convertor and B&M hi-performance bands — all operated by a 'Quick-Click' ratchet shifter.

Pumping Rubber

BRACKET RACING

As you can see, class racing is based on fairly tight guidelines — a car is usually built to fit into one specific class, will race against cars similar in both appearance and speed, and will rarely move into another class without major modifications. Comp Altereds look like Comp Altereds and race each other; Modified cars conform to the Modified rules and race the other Modifieds. But bracket racing is a completely different format of drag racing and cuts right across the class definitions.

At a race meeting organized on bracket lines there will be a number of brackets, usually about five, and probably called Top, Senior, Middle, Junior and Rookie, or some such labels, into which the competing cars are slotted by speed — quite regardless of their class, style, engine capacity, or any other consideration. The NDRC and the BDRA use class systems in the main and run bracket meetings only occasionally, while Pennine run bracket meets exclusively.

At a typical Pennine one-day meeting the time before lunch is given over to qualifying. Every competitor has to make at least one run and set a 'qualifying' time, which is automatically taken from his fastest run — there is no choice by the race driver or team as there would be on a dial-in within class racing.

During the lunch break the race controllers bracket together racers with similar times — at Pennine there are five brackets each for cars and bikes and one for trucks. For the sake of argument, the cars in Top bracket might all have been qualifying with times of 10 seconds or less, Senior might be around the 12s, Middle could be 13s and 14s, the 15s and 16s would comprise Junior, and anything in the 17s and slower would be in the Rookie bracket.

Any style of car, therefore, can end up running against virtually any other; flathead rails stage against street-legal machines, Pro Comp cars can meet big Yanks that might have been in Production in class racing.

At the start of eliminations, after lunch, Middle bracket — to take just one — might consist of seven racers. This will mean four races in the first round; three full-bore paired racers and one lucky chap getting a bye. After all the brackets have run their first rounds, the surviving four racers in Middle will pair-up in two races for the second round. The third round will be the final between the two remaining cars. Pairing systems vary, and can result in the fastest car in the bracket meeting the slowest immediately — as you'll see later on in the book. Pennine do not build any advantage into the lights either; the race cars get their greens simultaneously. This has led to criticism that the fastest car in the bracket — leaving aside break-outs and red-lighting — is bound to win. For this reason the racers are allowed some flexibility with a 0.5 break-out margin. The argument on the other hand is that the guy who has persuaded his car to go the fastest deserves to win; what lawyers would call a 'nice' distinction. In practice, this means that you win at a bracket meeting by taking care to stay within the bracket which you feel you can dominate and by running consistently. There might well be

The American style of storming bracket racer. This glass-fibre-bodied Willys coupe was imported in the summer of 1980, but was beset by bad luck and grenaded motors. By the end of 1981, though, the Willys had grown to a blown 426-ci Hemi.

no more than a tenth of a second between the top qualifier in Middle bracket and in with a great chance, or being the slowest qualifier in Junior and being seen off as a matter of routine in the first round.

So with 11 brackets and at least seven races over the three rounds in each bracket, spectators are guaranteed 77 races after lunch, which gives a clue to the evolution of this system of dragging.

Some race classes are more popular than others, some are more fashionable and some can simply get too expensive. A few years back the top American drag promoters got together and devised the Bracket format as a way of adapting to the fact that certain classes were shrinking and the class system couldn't cope with the increased interest in what we would know as Street and Production.

To a large degree the same is true over here; a thinly populated class such as Production might produce so few competitors at a meeting that the whole thing might be over with a single race. Obviously, this would be an

A home-grown bracket bomber from Bradford. Neil Harker's immaculate Falcon looks good and goes well. In class racing it would run in Street.

unhappy state of affairs for all concerned — racers, spectators and promoters.

Bracket racing is at its most successful with people such as Pennine; the format works best for what I hope I'll be forgiven for calling the lower two-thirds (in performance terms) of British racers, and that is the area for which Pennine principally caters. Bracket racing does nothing for Funny Car pilots and can be of no advantage to them; it works well, though, with a field of Competition Altereds, Production and Street cars — providing frequent and competitve racing and adding new dimensions, as well as a greater opportunity for a driver to become a winner.

Steve Murty, of Pennine Promotions, explains further: 'The overwhelming advantage of bracket racing is that a newcomer can read the magazines, get the bug and start in drag racing with something like a home-built Comp Altered. If you're consistent you can be competitive and start winning very soon. In class racing you have to be immediately competitive against very experienced drivers who have probably worked their way up through the classes — and it's very difficult to catch up on these experienced racers; often at a class meeting you can look through the programme and tell in advance who's going to win. With bracket racing you never know who you're going to race against until you've qualified.

'Also, you can run less highly strung vehicles and win with a strong reliable car. You don't need to blow your engine up, but can have a good day's racing and out-drive the opposition by using your head rather than the car.

'The criticism that's always levelled at bracket racing is sandbagging — that the competitors never try to go faster. I completely disagree — if only because it's human nature. Racers can't just sit there and not try to go faster. It's a fact that most people don't win because they want to go *too* fast.

A Junior Comp Altered by construction, but a bracket car by usage. Dave South-worth's Rover V8-engined Jeep sports a home-made aluminium body.

Steven Tong takes full advantage of bracket racing's potential, and when he's not racing his Volvo truck he's competing on two wheels. The bike in the picture has subsequently been replaced by the ex-Pip Higham machine.

'To get round the sandbagging charge, though, we've just introduced a rule that a car's best ever time carries forward — so that you can never back-track unless there are special circumstances or new modifications.

'The key is consistency. The cool customer will always out-drive the opposition. In brackets you've got to drive well. In class racing you can drive a good car badly and win — in bracket racing it's always a race from the word go.'

Chain Reaction

BIKE DRAGGING

It's rare indeed to find a single motor sport which manages to successfully cater for both two-wheeled and four-wheeled competitors and enthusiasts, but drag racing has done exactly that right from the start and virtually every drag meeting in this country offers the sights and sounds of both cars and bikes on the same track within minutes of each other. Can you imagine autocross drivers sharing their venues with trials riders? Or Formula One cars road racing on the Isle of Man?

There is, one must admit, the occasional grumble from drag bike riders about their second-place billing and the feeling that they are perhaps a second string to the racing bow, but by and large drivers and riders are quite at peace, realizing that the breadth of interest provided by a more varied day's racing not only increases the size of the crowd and that crowd's enjoyment, but invariably wins them converts from the other ranks, too. No drag car fanatic can turn away from one of the all-too-terrifying looking bike duels, and what dyed-in-the-leather biker is really going to sneer at a 6-second Pro Comp full-power pass?

This book is about drag racing as a sport, and within that definition it majors on four-wheeled dragging rather than two, but this isn't merely a token chapter — nor does bike dragging need a book to itself as I had first thought. The truth is that the two aspects of the one sport do have so much in commom that a vast amount of this book, although written about cars, can be applied in essence to bike dragging, too.

The origins of American and European bike dragging differ. From the earliest days in the United States bikes and cars simply raced each other; what a sight — a high boy in one lane and a stripped-down Harley-Davidson in the other! Given limited power plants — the native V-twins and British singles and parallel-twins — the American bike racers soon started looking around for heftier motivation.

Ed Potter wasn't called The Michigan Madman for nothing. He took a more than somewhat modified Harley frame and an injected Corvette engine and bolted the two together. As Tom Wolfe noted in his book *The Pump House Gang,* Ed had trouble getting a clutch system sorted out, so his mechanic would lift the back wheel up while Ed found a gear, and then simply drop the thing on to the asphalt once the revs were right and watch it go fishtailing madly up the quarter.

Tom Reisner followed in Potter's footsteps. He created Tom's Bomb, a 550-lb Chevrolet V8 in a 300-lb H-D 74 frame. Really. And the moonlit nights of 1961 saw him making test runs on the then half-constructed Route 71 outside Newark, Ohio. The experiments continued on the American strips throughout that decade... hardly *that* bizarre, though, when you think what the factory teams were getting up to with the early Funny Cars at the same time.

British bike dragging, meanwhile, was developing through altogether more respectable channels. Sprinting was, and is, a test of acceleration where a competitor races against the clock rather than an opponent. There

Rod Pallant on a blown single-engined Harley David-son Leviathan at Santa Pod in the early-Seventies.

were four or five well-known British bike sprinting venues of which the most famous was the bumpy ride down the parade beneath the prom at Brighton. The sport was dominated for many years by George Brown and his supercharged 997-cc Vincent, Super Nero. In the mid-Sixties a goodly number of the guys who had been chasing George's laurels widened their interest to the emerging sport of drag racing. Norman Hyde was one such, as was Alf Hagon, who took British bike dragging times into single figures in the summer of '67 with a 9.679 on his V-twin 1,100-cc nitro-powered Hagon-Jap.

The legendary George Brown, astride a blown Triumph, uses a set of rollers powered by his van's rear wheel, to fire up the bike.

Rod Pallant's 1981 mount was aptly named Heavy Metal in recognition of the Buick/Rover V8 which has been slipped into the frame.

A dummy headlamp and the shocker-replacement struts with wheelie bars are the only external give-aways to this street bike's drag trim. A steadying hand is aiding a burnout.

The pattern of occasional bike-only meetings within a basic format of car-and-bike meets with the classes running off alternately was established and has survived, but on two wheels just about everything else has changed. The scruffy matt-black leathers with the baggy seats are now rare. The 'pudding basin' helmets worn with goggles have long since disappeared. The top drag bike racers of the Eighties are well turned-out, frequently run very smart teams, and are as much crowd-pleasing showmen as the top Funny Car and rail pilots.

The revolution, though — the one factor which makes the marques of bikes listed as winners at the BDRA's first-ever Motorcycle Drag Championship . . . Vincent, Rudge, Norton, BSA, Francis Barnett . . . as much a piece of history as if they'd been push-bikes — was the arrival of the Japanese motorcycle.

Even 10 to 12 years ago, when I was the most enthusiastic biker you could meet, my staple diet — and that of my mates — was machinery such as the Norton Dominator, the Triumph Bonneville and the BSA Gold Star. There were Honda 4s around, of course, but only in the way that TR7 drivers notice that some folk own Mazda RX7s . . . foreign oddities, a different style of things, something a touch suspicious which needed to be kept at arm's length.

The British drag bikes are still around and still competitive, but the injection of multi-cylindered Japanese machinery forced standards and speeds to staggering levels. Out of 114 American National Motorcycle Racing Association drag class records, eight are held by Triumphs, five by Harley Davidsons, two by BSAs — and all the rest by Japanese bikes. Top of the pile, in the Stateside Top Fuel bike class, are Bo O'Brochta and Russ Collins — Bo with a best ever ET of 7.08 on a Kawasaki, and Russ with a terminal record of 199.55 mph on his twin-engined Honda. Back over this side, Henk Vink was the first guy to dip into the 7s in Europe when he ran 7.802 at Drachten, in his native Holland, in August 1980. His machine? Japanese — a ferocious twin-engined blown Kawasaki, prepared by Kenny Annesley, at Motorcycles Unlimited, in Oklahoma. The Swedish rider Stefan Reisten took his blown 1,000-cc Honda to Santa Pod in September '80 and put down a record 7.87 at 174 mph — the fastest time on British tarmac — while the fastest Briton at the time of writing is Jeff Byne, whose 8.02 on his blown double-engined Triumph is an exception to the rule of

Nigel Patrick's 1,200-cc turbo Kawasaki, Drag Specialities, which features a frame by chop-builder Uncle Bunt, and runs in Pro Fuel.

'Put the kettle on, Mum, I'm coming 'ome.' Everything I've said in this book about the critical moment of the launch certainly applies as much to bikes as it does to cars.

An occupational hazard for bikers. Wheelies don't help a run, especially when they get this high. A few more degrees of lift and the air resistance could have forced this rider off.

The VBS Suzuki CBX Pro Stocker is typical of the breed. This new class got off to a very promising start in 1981.

Japanese supremacy.

There are three basic divisions for drag bikes — Street (denoted by the letter S before the race number), Pro Street (PS) and Competition (C), plus two additional divisions which merely dictate the fuel of a Comp bike; Gas Competition (G) for petrol-burning engines, and Methanol Competition (M) for meths drinkers.

The classes within these divisions are broken down by capacity (measured in cc, not cubic inches):

AA	–	2,001-3,500 cc (unblown)
A	–	1,301-2,000 cc
B	–	1,001-1,300 cc
C	–	751-1,000 cc
D	–	501-750 cc
E	–	351-500 cc
F	–	240-350 cc

Thus, Michael Carter's beautiful Imperial Wizard, race number BPS 70, is a Pro Street bike of between 1,001 cc and 1,300 cc (1,198-cc Kawasaki in fact), and Eddy Lloyd's 2,250 double-milled Kawasaki Freight Train runs Gas Comp and carries the number AAG 20.

Street is open to all bikes which are fully street legal; taxed, tested and insured. All lights, instruments, speedo, electrical systems and exhausts must be working and street legal. Tyres and mudguards must be street items, too. The bike's frame must be factory issue, as must the suspension, but engine modifications are allowed and carbs, fuel pumps, gearbox and clutch are free of restrictions (but subject to safety regulations). Street bikes must run on petrol and cannot either be supercharged or have more than one engine. An ignition cut-off must be fitted on the top yoke of the handlebars, but cannot merely be a magneto-kill button. Drive chains must be guarded with 1/8-inch dural or the equivalent. Fuel tanks must be made of steel and the bike's stand must be either removed or securely wired up. Check the full BDRA or NDRC rule books for brake specifications.

Pro Street bikes are based on street machinery, but can be modified much more extensively. Only one engine may be used and that must be a generally available production bike engine. There are no limits on its modifications, though. Supercharging, turbocharging and fuel injection are all permitted. Guards are required on blower belt-drives. Pro Street bikes can run open headers providing the exhaust is directed well away from tyres and tank. The bike's frame must be based on a generally available item, be it one from a major manufacturer or a specialist supplier. Maximum wheelbase is 65 inches and minimum wheel diameter 16 inches. Front tyres must be at least 2.75 inches wide while slicks are allowed on the back to a maximum width of 4 inches. The front suspension must operate, but although the rear suspension must appear to be present it need not actually function. Front and rear lights must be fitted, but do not need to work. tion. Front and rear lights must be fitted, but do not need to work. Horns, generators and other electrical equipment are not required. All other regulations are as for Street.

These two classes are where the clever guys run faster by careful reading of the rule book. Dummy items, such as seats and tanks, are common weight-saving tricks. Street bikes may run with internally shortened forks which lower the bike, and with tiny batteries. Pro Street riders can take the concept even further — anything inoperative, but obligatory, will be a flimsy dummy item.

Competition bikes are just that — machines built for all-out racing. The bike's frame can be constructed or altered as the rider requires, but must be of tubular-frame construction. Butt-welds must be reinforced and welds must not be excessively ground. It is not permitted to use the engine as a major stress member. Any internal combustion engine is allowed, with any modification, and fuel is free of restriction. Cast flywheels are not allowed — they must be steel (applicable where car engines are being used) and blower drives must be guarded. Supercharging is not taken into account for the purposes of classification. Exhausts are as for Pro Street and suspension,

In between rounds, Henk Vink's Dutch crew work on his monstrous double-engined Kawasaki.

wheelbase and wheels are free. A minimum ground clearance of 3 inches is recommended. Positive on/off switches are obligatory, as are fuel shut-offs on Comp bikes running nitro. Batteries and electrical equipment are at the rider's discretion.

In addition, there are a number of general bike safety rules. Fuel lines must be securely fitted and must include an on/off tap. Bikes must be equipped with overflow chambers of at least ½-pint capacity from the oil breather. All drain plugs must be wire-locked. Steering stops must be fitted in such a way that there is at least one inch between the handlebars and the tank on full lock, and the bars must be able to move through at least 20 degrees to either side of the central line. Grips must be firmly attached and the levers must be of the ball-ended type. Only twist grips are allowed for operating the throttle and they must close automatically when released. No

Steve Tong launches hard and pulls a modest wheelie on the turbocharged Orient Express Kawasaki, which he imported from the States. Running on gas, he's within a hair's width of 7 s.

65

device which lifts the rear wheel from the ground at the start-line is allowed.

Where a fairing or streamlining is fitted it must be made of metal, glass-fibre, or similar flameproof material. It must allow the rider complete liberty of movement at all times and must give 2 inches of clearance between it and the handlebars, nor must it come into contact with the front wheel at any time.

An ACU helmet must be worn, with goggles or a visor of non-splintering material. Clothing must be a leather one-piece suit. Boots must not have exposed metal plates of any sort and must overlap the bottom of the trousers by at least 2 inches. Clothing must be in good condition, and like the bike, be 'presented for scrutineering in a clean and tidy condition'. Not just so's your mum's proud of you, either!

At the time of writing, the decision had been made to introduce a Pro Stock Formula One bike class for the '81 season. This is a sort of super Pro Street class which has been operating very successfully in the United States, with guys like Bob Carpenter and Terry Vance running high-8s on bikes which, as the rules state, must be of stock appearance from a distance of 50 feet. Terry's best time to date in Pro Stock is an 8.70, running gas with an octane booster, but without a blower or a turbo.

The class could well develop with considerable ferocity in Europe and be one of bike dragging's biggest attractions within a very short space of time. The rules allow very high technology and a virtually unlimited amount of engineering expertise, but the class retains a street-real identity.

One guy who has done more than his fair share to establish Pro Stock is Pip Higham, of The Village Bike Shop, in Manchester. Backed by Heron Suzuki GB, Texaco, *SuperBike* magazine and the like, Pip is a sponsor's dream — a showman and a winner. His Pro Stocker is a Suzuki GSX with around 160 bhp behind the twist grip. Pip launches the bike — which is known as The Deuce for some obscure reason — at 8,000 revs and shifts via a very advanced compressed air-operated system which, through an air solenoid and an electrical kill switch, drops the ignition for eight-hundreths of a second while the compressed air forces a foolproof clutchless shift.

The Pro Stocker's stablemate and silver-black-and-red team companion is the SuzuperBike turbocharged B-class gasser, which can lay claim to a best-ever time of 9.00/152 from 1,176 cc. Pip, incidentaly, holds the world Street class record at 9.94/142.8 — which is going more than slightly.

At Pennine Drag Racing Club meets the bikes run off in brackets in exactly the same way as the cars (and trucks).

Bikes are as refined and specialized a branch of dragging as are the cars. Indeed, some would argue that to prepare and campaign a successful drag bike in a Competition division requires as much expertise, application and cash as to field a top Comp Altered car. On the other hand, though, just as it is possible to drag a Street car on a budget, it is certainly easier to bring out your Street bike and start racing competitively. As you'll see later in the book, when we look at building a car engine for dragging, the key is strength and reliability. Speed, more speed, and yet more speed can be found through expertise or a widely-opened wallet — or both — but a little practice, careful planning and a large degree of riding skill... or at least the ability to learn... are the most valuable assets to see you safely embarked on a bike dragging career.

Staging, Holeshooting, Shifting and Shutdowns

RACE PROCEDURE

'What actually happens at a drag strip when you first arrive — what's the procedure?' I was asked that, again, by a would-be competitor recently and, as I can well appreciate that there is nothing worse than arriving as a complete newcomer and being all too nervous of displaying one's ignorance, I think it's worth spelling out the basic routine and the all-important start-line procedure. All this is straightforward and theoretical, as it were. In the next chapter you will be able to see how things work out for real.

When you arrive at the strip, the first thing to do is to move away from the spectators' lane and enter by the separate competitors' gate — at SPR you go straight on when others turn left, at Long Marston you keep over to the left as soon as you leave the main road, at Pennine you stay to the right and then go straight on under the pylons. (Check out the maps at the back of the book for details of the strips themselves.)

Find yourself an area which you can call your pits. Don't crush in too tight on others and if there's obviously a tow car and/or a trailer parked up allow them room to bring their race car back. Catch your breath, stand on an oil can and have a good look round, then sign on at race control and get your car scrutineered by the RAC official, having already fitted your slicks or whatever. Having been allowed a race number it must be clearly displayed on both sides of the car in letters and figures at least 6 inches high.

From there it's up to you, in your own time, to make your way to the staging lanes where a marshal will direct you to a queue of waiting cars (if no marshal is on duty just pull up behind a car which looks as if it belongs to your class). The schedule for qualifying varies; at a one-day meeting it's from about 10.00 am until lunch (usually 1.00 or 1.30 pm) and then eliminations start after a break of about one hour. At a two-day event the first day is given over completely to qualifying, and the eliminations (the racing proper) take place on the second day. At a three-day meet — exclusively SPR events at the moment — the first day is for all racers to qualify with the exception of Pro-Fuel and Funny Car, the second day is qualifying for Pro-Fuel and Funny Car and eliminations for everyone else, while the last day is eliminations for all — with those who have already raced their quickest ETs from the first and second days.

You can put in as many qualifying passes as you like, and time allows. At your first meet go for, say, three — maybe four if you arrived early. If you make adjustments in between your runs keep them simple. Some strips have 'play pens' out in the boondocks where you can fire up in safety to test the efficiency of any mods before coming back to the staging lanes.

When you get to the front of the queue in the staging lanes a marshal will direct you to pull forward and indicate against whom he is pairing you. The pairing in qualifying is quite random and do not be tempted to try too hard to race him. It doesn't matter who crosses the finish line first; all you want to do is feel how your car is running, look and listen for problems and establish a qualifying time. (You must make at least one qualifying run.)

The early birds line up for scrutineering at New York and 'Dirty' Des Taylor is having trouble with his hood catches. The strip itself stretches out to the top right.

The staging lanes at Mantorp Park. This is the place for chatting, comparing times and doing a lot of waiting around.

The marshal's signs will be fairly self-evident, but if you are at all confused beckon him over to you (preferable to driving up to him and perhaps getting tangled with other cars) and ask his help. Some folk use their shoe white and write 'rookie' on the screen; no bad idea.

Anyone signed on as a mechanic may come down into the fire-up lane behind the start-line — though marshals may object to more than one or two mechanics. They must not be in the car when you stage or race. If you are using a push car it must stay back out of the way once your racer's engine is running and can proceed down the strip after you when waved on by a marshal. The only other reason for it to move is if you've lost fire and there is time for you to be repushed. (All that is only applicable to non-self-starting cars without cooling systems — the push car bump-starts the racer

and then tows it back along the return road after the race.)

If you lose fire on the start-line and cannot restart, the car must be pushed back to the fire-up lane as quickly as possible. If you lose fire some way down the strip, after a long burnout for example, then the car must be pushed as far as possible off the track and the driver must get out of the car and get over the crash barrier before the other race car can run. No-one can run in a lane where there is an abandoned vehicle.

If you are going to go in for a burnout it must be done in the allocated spot and excessive water may not be used. If this is your first run I would suggest giving the burnouts a miss. Take care not to drive through any pools of water left by previous burnouts — water on your tyres will lose you valuable traction.

With your motor running, your safety harness buckled-up, your crash helmet strapped on, and — where appropriate — your side windows wound right up, the start-line marshal will then beckon you forward. (The one direction from a marshal that is more important than any other is when he mimes a throat-cutting operation — that means that he knows something that you do not and you must switch off your engine immediately.)

Now we meet the christmas tree. To paraphrase the BDRA regs, the functions of the christmas tree and the control system are six-fold. It indicates when a race car has correctly staged (got into the precise position), it activates the start-light sequence which also has a facility for a handicap in one lane to be dialled in, it indicates when a foul start has taken place, it

The christmas tree. It can look very confusing at first, but if you've watched it in operation as a spectator it should be self-explanatory.

indicates (at most strips) which car or bike has crossed the finishing line first, it measures the elapsed time between tripping of the start and finish beams (the ET) and it measures the average terminal speed of the car or bike as it crosses the finish line. The system in each lane is quite identical yet independent.

Christmas trees vary slightly, but on average have seven lights for each lane, mounted vertically. They function from top to bottom. Roll forward slowly into stage, your hand on the handbrake, ready. There are three light beams on the ground which stretch between two units. You are in stage when your front wheels are breaking the middle beam and the large non-flashing light of the top three on the christmas tree illuminates. The top light will come on and flash if you are too far back, and the bottom one of those three will light up and flash if you are too far forward. Approach slowly and nudge into stage. The marshal will assist you. If you roll too far forward, reverse back a couple of feet and try again.

After the guy in the other lane is correctly staged you have 20 seconds to get into stage yourself (though this is sometimes at the discretion of race control) and on some christmas trees the big red light at the bottom will start flashing slowly to warn you that you are taking too long; the flashing will get quicker until the 20 seconds are up and will then stay on. This disqualifies you. If you are disqualified by a red light, go ahead with the race anyway — don't try to pull back.

With your stage light smiling forth, hold the car on the handbrake, and keep your thumb over the sprung button so that you can drop it quickly (some racers without 'fly-off' racing handbrakes tape over the sprung button to avoid engaging on the ratchet). Stay calm. Don't let yourself get flustered. Don't pay too much attention to the guy in the other lane — likewise his set of lights. Concentrate on getting things right for yourself and watch those lights — after three or four passes you'll get the pace of them okay.

Experienced racers have their tricks. Obviously a front tyre can be just cutting the beam by rolling into it, or can be 10 inches or so further forward so they've just about left it. The former is called 'shallow staging' and

The timing lights which throw a beam across the start-line. These are linked to the three lights at the top of the christmas tree. Let the marshal help you into stage, and then just take it easy.

The staging lights need something positive to cancel the beam, so bikes and dragsters with wire front wheels are often fitted with a staging hoop. This wheel alone would be too narrow to properly break the beam and the car could roll out of stage with the tiniest movement.

provides a small amount of leeway for you to roll forward. If you roll forward out of the beam before your green light comes on, your red light will illuminate and disqualify you. Some racers, though, stage shallow and allow for various split-seconds in their reaction times and in the actual car itself as it launches, and with their few inches of extra roll, start to launch as soon as the last amber light has gone out — gambling on the car's front wheel not actually leaving the stage beam until the green 'go' light has come on.

But I leap ahead somewhat. You're in stage. If you've had to reverse to restage, check that you're in first gear. Lift the clutch pedal until you can just feel it biting, and take the gas pedal slowly down until the rev counter gives you the engine speed which practice has told you is a safe optimum launch speed. Coming down the tree there will be two, or very occasionally three, amber lights and then a single green. The ambers will come on one after another; when the green lights up, get away. Let the handbrake right

The timing equipment in race control. The central unit controls the lights and any handicap which needs to be dialled-in, while those on either side record the ETs in each lane, together with the terminal speeds.

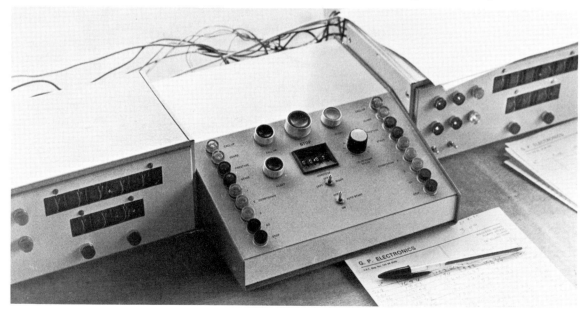

off and ease the clutch and accelerator — don't jump off the clutch on to the gas, or you'll bog the motor. Easy does it, as the expression goes.

You're on your way. Shift quickly and cleanly on your rev peaks, and as you cross the finish-line you may find yourself ahead of the other car; the winner is the guy who crosses the line first. ETs and terminal speeds are incidentals, purely of academic interest (indeed it is possible to beat a car which has a faster ET if you get away from the lights quicker).

The finish area covers 132 feet, with light beams on the finish-line and both 66 feet before it and 66 feet beyond it. These last two are the terminal speed recorders which compute your average speed between those points.

You may see brake lights shining before a car has reached the finish-line and a subsequent very low terminal speed. If a racer is fairly certain that he has a good lead over his opponent, but may be running close to his break-out, he will spend as much time playing with his brakes at the top end of the strip as he did with his accelerator at the start-line. However, it's easy to lose races doing that if you can't judge it dead right.

Having crossed the finish-line, slow down gradually and turn into the return road (a left turn at the Pod and Long Marston, a right turn at New York), avoid driving into the other racer while giving him a cheery wave, and return to the pits or the other end of the staging lanes. Along the way you will be presented with a small ticket upon which your ET and terminal speed will have been written.

The pairings for the eliminations will be announced over the PA (and sod's law states that someone near you will always fire his motor up and take it to maximum revs just as your race number is mentioned) and/or be posted up at race control. It's then up to you to get next to your first opponent in the pairing lane and await the call to arms. This tends to be drag racing's biggest social gathering, and by far the best place to hear the gossip and exchange malicious rumours.

If you survive your first pairing, the process is repeated. These waits in the staging lanes, I should warn you, can be lengthy. In a successful afternoon's racing you may enjoy a total of one minute's competition and not enjoy two hours of traffic jam behind the start-line, and sod's law also goes on to state that if you are working on your motor in the staging lanes the marshals will call you up when everything is undone or disconnected.

Drag races tend to be lost rather than won, and apart from the other guy crossing the line first there are a number of ways a race can be lost. As I've mentioned, getting a red for a foul start or failing to get into stage will lose you your race, as will the failure to make it to the start-line — no matter how good your excuse for not meeting your pairing, race control is unlikely to let you run (though if you've a strong case and a good reason it is sometimes worth a polite argument). Crossing the centre-line will lose you your race, as, of course, will breaking-out in a bracket race. Every club also has a reckless-driving or conduct-unbecoming rule, related to your doing anything which might bring the sport into disrepute or endanger someone's safety. Anyone under the influence of alcohol or drugs is likely to be banned from racing if his abilities seem impaired.

An item of procedure which is worth running through — but which I hope you will never come across — concerns protests. If you consider that a competitor is cheating in any way you can protest in writing to either the Clerk of the Course or the Race Controller. The protest note must be accompanied by a fee of £10 for cars (£50 at an international meeting) and £1 for bikes (£20 at an international). This fee will be returned to you if your protest is upheld, but is otherwise forfeited.

Any protest concerning race classifications must be made before eliminations start, and any protest concerning a race must be made within half-an-hour of the results being announced.

The procedure is as follows. The car or bike which is the subject of the protest will be taken out of competition and its paired opponent will run a bye. To quote the BDRA rule book: 'After the class elimination has been completed the protested vehicle will race against the winner of the elimination at that point. After the race the disputed vehicle will be checked

PENNINE DRAG RACING CLUB
New York Raceway

Certificate of Speed

TIME   AM/PM

DATE: ELAPSED TIME

RACE No. 551

TERMINAL SPEED   109 LOSE

The verdict. The timing ticket gives the ET, and should also record the date and time of the run, but the vital piece of information is that win/lose note scrawled in the bottom corner!

for classification.'

If the protest is upheld then this last race is nullified. If the protest is not proved then the examined vehicle is the class winner. Any race points or prize money earned by the guy who made the protest will pass to the slandered racer. If a protest is upheld then the cheating driver must pay the examination costs, but if the protest is found to be groundless the costs will fall upon the protester.

DAYS IN THE DRAG RACING SCENE

Theory; smashing in itself, but likely to let you down badly when you try to use it to prop up reality. Having written all this about how to go drag racing the only thing to do next was to take a stock motor and enter the brackets.

There were three of us, Dennis, Alastair and me. We had all raced before but, as at every meeting, there was a lot to be learned. The car we took was an 'Indy Race Car Replica' Mustang borrowed from Removatop, but it could have been anything. The race meeting we entered was at Pennine's New York Dragway, near York.

The preliminary work was simple. We obtained Restricted Speed competition licences from the RAC and entered the car for the day by contacting Pennine's Competition Secretary (all addresses can be found at the end of the book). The car itself is very slightly larger and rather heavier than a Ford Capri. It is powered by a 302ci V8 with one 2-barrel carb. The gearbox is a 3-speed with an overdrive as fourth gear.

As Dennis and I drove up to Cheshire to meet Alastair we started learning some of the car's limitations. The Federal emission control was stifling the engine, which was torquey, but never seemed to really get hold of the power potential. It was under-carbed and the gear spread was far from ideal. Also, on our car, third gear selection was fading away. It was obvious that it would not stand up to racing, so we decided that we would have to live without it and either run the quarter in first and second, or virtually sandbag into overdrive.

The big disability, though, was the rear-end set-up. Although it was a coil-and-shocks system, it was very soft and the car tramped badly.

At an undisclosed location in North Cheshire (as they say) we spent the midnight hours of the Friday dragging the car over a roughly measured quarter-mile. It was looking like a 17 or 18-second machine — and we were starting to have second thoughts about entering it at all. The launch was all-important with the spongey rear; all too easily the car would sit and smoke or simply bounce its axle alarmingly. There was nothing we could do about that — ladder bars and air shocks would probably have solved the problem completely, but we had no mandate to go to such lengths on someone else's car. It would all be down to practice and attempts at consistency. The other insuperable problem was weight — it would not have been difficult to get rid of a significant amount of dead weight, but for the same reason that was out of the question.

The following day, the Saturday, was the *Hot Car*/Russell Performance Products Street Racing Championship at New York. Dennis and I got over there early and decided that we would have nothing to lose by entering the Mustang in that. We weren't likely to break, our times wouldn't qualify us for the following day's racing, and we could simply regard it all as good practice.

Dennis signed on as driver and made several passes, coming out — to our great surprise — with a best time of 15.65. Really very respectable.

The next day we again arrived at the strip in good time. We found

OFFICIAL PACE CAR
63rd ANNUAL INDIANAPOLIS 500 MILE RACE MAY 27, 1979

DIW 3523

Dennis and the Removatop Mustang await the scrutineer's judgment as he delves deep. I wonder if Dennis would be tempted to let go of the hood if he got a 'No'?

ourselves some pit space and started to unload our luggage from the Mustang. That ran us into our first big problem — no support car. As Alastair hadn't arrived yet we had nowhere to put our tools, luggage, camera cases and all the other stuff which was packed in the Muzzie. A tent would have been a good enough store, but as it was we had to stuff our chattels into the cars of a couple of friends. How these guys who drive to the strip, race and drive home manage it, I don't know; an overnight stay would certainly make that very difficult.

Next stop was the scrutineer's caravan. He checked the car over thoroughly and pronounced it healthy, though he wasn't happy with the fact that we had forgotten our proper 1-kg fire extinguisher and only had a small aerosol.

A look under the Mustang's hood revealed a great mass of smog plumbing. We were worried that we would upset the overall balance of the

DIW 3523

Removing the Mustang's exhaust system was a perilous two-man, one-woman operation and is hardly to be recommended. A cut-out would have done the job for us.

75

engine if we took too much off, but made a start and broke up the system by simply removing the air filter lid and element. At this stage we had a look at the exhaust system. That was where the greatest single gain could obviously be made, but for the time being we did no more than look.

Time to make our first qualifying run. We had a good look round at the opposition, and soon realized that life wasn't going to be easy. The field was smaller than usual and half a dozen of the 16 and 17-second cars I would have expected to have seen were absent. We took a good look at what there was and tried to work out how hard we would have to run to stay ahead of a bracket. The only way we were in with a chance was to keep the Mustang's times low and try and ease ourselves into top position in the slowest bracket. With the poor back-end we couldn't bank on fast times, even though the car might be capable of them.

Dennis made the first qualifying pass and logged a reasonable 17.50; at that, the rear wheels were hopping and smoking off the line. Another look around and we decided that if we could coax the car to a lower 17 — say 17.2 — and were able to stay there, then we might qualify as the fastest car in Rookie bracket.

The trick, as you can see, is not necessarily to be fastest, but to be consistent, and with our car the driving skills were all-important. Dumping the clutch and hitting the gas, for example, was no way to get off the line — nothing would happen and you'd sit there burning rubber. The pedals had to be feathered.

Dennis went out for a second qualifier, but got no time because — uncharacteristically, I must say — he red-lighted, and it's worth reciting why. As he pulled forward to the line, a cigarette packet had bounced up from under the seat. Now it lodged beneath the pedal as he staged, and shifting the pedal pressure to kick it out of the way was just enough to roll out of stage and pull a cherry. Silly, yes, but that could have been a final we'd lost rather than just a qualifier.

Another unknown quantity was the pressure in the rear tyres. We did try taking them down by 5 psi, but only trial and error could give us a satisfactory answer — very difficult to judge when the suspension was giving us such launch problems.

By now it was noon. There was little qualifying time left and, more than slightly late, Alastair arrived. We had promised him the day's driving and, true to our word, we got him signed on and, having briefed him extensively, sent him out for a run. His time was 17.8, which was reasonable (and times apply to the car not the driver, so the Mustang was still dialled in at 17.5) but we sent him out again.

What we discovered now was that you don't change drivers in the middle of a day's racing. Alastair had not had enough time with the car and couldn't appreciate the traction problems that we had discovered. He ran 16.76, which moved our dial-in too high and put us into Junior Car as the slowest qualifier.

We had already dismissed the mid-15 as a virtual fluke and realized that the only way we could stay competitive would be to make the car go faster — so that mid-16s were the rule rather than the exception. The danger, of course, was that we might have to run very close to our break-out speed.

We spent a hard lunch break removing the car's exhaust system. Not easy; we had to virtually remove the back axle to get it off, and at one point we were using no less than three borrowed trolley jacks.

We finished work just in time to take the car to the 'play pen', a large empty area beyond the pits. The thing was certainly breathing much better and revving more freely, and losing the exhaust had not upset the carb settings.

Having returned to the pits we made some final adjustments and I fired the Muzzie up again to drive round to the pairing lanes. The mill spluttered and died. Consternation in the camp. Then realization that we'd run out of petrol. Yes, such elementary things do get overlooked. The rub was that our spare can was inside the friend's car, and she'd locked herself out; yet another silly circumstance which could have lost us a vital race. Just in time,

we were able to get into the car and retrieve our petrol.

Then the bitterest blow. We checked the pairings and found that we were drawn against the fastest car in the bracket. The difference in times was well over a second — so unless he did something silly, such as breaking-out or red-lighting, there was no way we could beat him without breaking-out.

All our work had been in vain. But, of course, that's the way it goes. I told Alastair to work at a holeshot — shave an amber if necessary and if he got ahead to stay ahead by the barest distance. On the other hand, I told him, if the Firebird we were drawn against came off the line strong he was to give it the works and break-out. Rather give an opponent a bad time and go home with a neat number on the timing slip rather than be seen to give up.

Because of the back-end problems we'd been launching the car from low revs — no more than 1,800 — but with water on the tyres from accidentally driving through somebody else's burnout area, and by launching at about 2,500, the green light saw Alastair sitting there with his rear tyres spinning and smoking. His time was 16.81 and the Firebird was long gone. That was just 16.81 seconds of competition, and it was now time to pack up and start the 250-mile drive home.

One lesson we did learn, though, was the value of a team manager; having someone who wasn't driving and who could stand and watch the car and work out what was going on. It was up to him then to make the decisions and formulate the policies. Sounds grand, I know, but it's smarter than guesswork.

There was also the lessons we had learnt and which we wanted to apply to our next bracket or Street class race meeting. On the long drive home we also checked off each hassle. These fell into several different areas; our approach and the slickness of our operation, the physical limitations of the car we were using and its particular weaknesses, the ability to 'read' bracket make-up and apply tactics accordingly, and the sheer experience — or lack of it — of ourselves as drivers, mechanics, or team managers. All of which may sound as if we were getting our 16-second car way out of proportion, but if you don't try to get it right you'll only spend a lot of time getting it wrong; and a problem is a problem whether your ETs are in the teens or in single figures.

The next thing had to be class racing, and a chance to apply our heavily analyzed experiences. We chose to enter an NDRC meet at their Long Marston strip near Stratford-On-Avon, three weeks after our bash at New York with the Removatop Mustang.

I telephoned the ever-helpful Frances Parker, of the NDRC, was dutifully ticked off for entering late, and received a great bundle through the post first thing the next morning. This was to be our first excursion into class

Mustangs old and new meet on the line and provide a study in styles as the 1980 Removatop Muzzie faces competition from a 351-ci Boss from the late-Sixties.

Our entry for the Long Marston meeting was this beautiful 3-litre Capri S kindly loaned by Barry Reynolds, Press Fleet Administrator for Ford UK.

racing and, reading the forms in bed as I supped my morning Earl Grey, I noticed some pertinent differences.

We were entering a 3-litre Ford Capri for Street. The NDRC sends out a very helpful information sheet on the class, and this pointed out, for instance, that the Mk 1 Capri was a good example of a car which did not have a firewall between the fuel tank and the passenger compartment — not a problem for us as ours was a later-style hatchback. I was only going to have to mark the ignition switch positions and colour the live battery lead yellow, as we had on the Mustang.

The sheet also told us how the NDRC run their Street class. You establish your ET in qualifying, and can then decide on your own 'dial-in' time — so you will run against any other car in Street with a handicap built into the lights. This means that if we dialled in at 16.5, and duly wrote that on the car's screen, and staged against a car running 15.8, then we would get a greeen light in our lane 0.7 second before the green lighted in our opponent's lane. In effect, the best and most consistent driver wins — almost regardless of the speed of his car.

Easy, you just dial-in high and let the handicap do all the work for you, yes? No. There is a zero break-out, so if you have dialled in at 16.5, you could disqualify yourself with even a 16.4. Hmmm, this wasn't going to be easy. Setting a balance on the dial-in and then running utterly consistently was going to be crucial. The Mustang with its vagueness would have been useless. Hopefully, the Capri, with better suspension, would be able to run a single figure again and again.

This was to be a two-day meeting, and the format was you could sign-on and be scrutineered from 10.30 am on the Saturday, and make qualifying runs from noon until 5 pm. Sunday you could sign-on from 8.00 am until noon, be scrutineered from 8.30 am until 11 am, and qualify from 9,30 am until 12.30 pm. The eliminations only took place after 1 pm on the Sunday.

We all arrived in good time — I had driven the Capri 3.0S from Surrey. This time we brought a borrowed frame tent, which was erected without delay in our pit area and served as an invaluable base and retreat, as well as overnight accommodation.

The only modifications we made to the car were to remove the air filter

cover and element, disconnect the power steering by simply removing the belt drive, and remove the exhausts to leave open headers. We had already marked the on/off ignition switch, labelled the battery leads, and secured our newly-acquired 1-kg fire extinguisher, and we went through scrutineering without any problems. Unlike Pennine meets, form at NDRC venues is to sign-on after scrutineering.

Dennis drove, and in the course of the Saturday afternoon we got in four qualifying runs. The first was only a tester, but 16.60 at 84 mph came up on the slip. Quite respectable. The Capri S's rear suspension and axle-locating system was greatly superior to that on the Mustang, and the car was launching beautifully.

Dennis was leaving the line at 2,000 revs, which meant no smoke, no wheelspin, just a clean launch, and was then power shifting at around 6,000 revs. The following runs gave times of 16.34, 16.45, and 16.43; the damp track was drying out, but didn't seem to be affecting us too much. This was looking good.

On the Sunday morning we got in one more qualifier. We took the rear tyre pressures to 22 psi on the left and 24 psi on the right and ran another 16.34.

Time to make a decision on the dial-in. On the one hand you don't want to be giving precious fractions of seconds away to the opposition, and yet you've got to be careful that you allow yourself some leeway and avoid breaking-out. We doubted that the Capri would better 16.30, and dialled in at that.

In the first round Dennis got a bye run and took it very easy. In the second round he was drawn up against an old Escort van with an 18.50 dial-in painted on its windows. It seems likely that with a lot of heavy machinery having gone down the strip (and this was only the second meeting on that tarmac), and with it having dried off so well by now, there was a lot of rubber down and the track itself had become faster. Bizarrely, the majority of the Street cars were breaking-out — and that's precisely what Dennis did; running a very fast time of 16.00. The irony was that the Escort van also broke-out — but because he broke-out by a smaller amount, he was awarded the race.

The Capri boasts a powerful and flexible engine, well located within a generous bay. We merely removed the exhausts and air cleaner, and the superior rear suspension set-up compared with the Muzzie was a great help for consistent and tidy launching.

79

I think the only lesson you can learn from that is that the number of variables in drag racing is infinite. The Capri was consistent and competitive, and while we had nailed down all the variables under our control, there were — and always will be — a number of factors about which we can do nothing at all. An auto box rather than a manual would have slowed us slightly, and might have made us more consistent — but the point is a touch academic. It was that time of the day again — time to refit the exhausts and start the long drive home.

Dreams of Glory

WHAT TO BUY AND RACE

Acquiring a basic car to run in the brackets, Street class, Production, or even Modified, need present no difficulty and need not cost very much at all. The first decision is which of the three classes I've just mentioned you want to aim for. Bracket racing has few of the set rules such as apply for class racing, so take the brackets for granted — the only variable will be which actual bracket your car's speed gets you into. Re-read the rules for Street, Production and Modified, check the styles and speeds of cars running in each class, and equate that to your budget. Even if you think right now that you're only interested in building yourself a bracket bomber, if your car ends up in between classes you are going to be ruling out a whole area of competition.

Bracket cars need not be, but Production cars must be (pretty well) street legal, and Street cars must, of course, have all the documents. Keeping a machine in street-legal trim is no great problem, but it is a point to decide early on. The biggest single job at this end of the market will be an engine swop; make the decision now. Engine transplants in Production are obviously the easiest as you are restricted to factory options. Modified will require major engine work. If you are nervous of swopping mills at this stage go for a big-engined car and aim for Street or Production.

Now give some thought to the style of car you want to end up with. If you build a Pop, paint it black and give it a flame job, everyone'll think you're trying to rip off Al's Gasser. You must establish your own identity, so stay away from anything that anyone else has done. Big Yanks certainly look the bit, but to be truly competitive they'll be expensive. Older cars, such as Jaguars, are very heavy, and a lot of that weight is detachable, so they are a good bet. Manufacturers often offered large engine options in old bodyshells after a few years of production — like the Vitesse from the Herald or the Tiger from the Alpine — another good bet; a fast car where all the drivetrain work involved in a mill swop has been done for you. Then again there are motors with their own character — how about a V6-powered Consul Capri to run in Street? Or a Street sleeping Hillman Hunter? Or a 3.3-litre Ventora to run in Production? Let alone a big-milled Modified Humber Hawk as a replica '55 Chevy?

Having decided more or less what style of basic car you're looking for, and whether you are going to be swopping engines straight off, you can now go hunting. Obviously, if you are going to sling the mill then you can look at machinery with dreadful power plants, not letting on what you want it for, point out the clouds of burning oil or whatever, and get the price down to your level. If you are going to keep the engine for at least a while, look at that first. You can accept some rust or body damage. MoT failures can be useful, too, depending, of course, on the reason for the failure.

Exchange and Mart is a handy market place, though prices in that worthy publication won't be the cheapest. Local papers are usually the best bet, and many have an 'Under £500' category. Car auctions are a good source of base material (stay away from the guys carrying tradeplates when they start

Your choice of basic car need not tend towards the exotic or fashionable. Mr Parr runs this Chevy-powered Australian Holden, which has been around in the UK for a long time, yet is still unique on these shores.

Getting into the exoticar league, Robin Stannard races his AC 3000 ME street car from time to time at New York.

bidding, though). If you are smart you can probably get to cars before they go to the block; approach friendly local dealers. They send to auction virtually everything over five years old and taken in part exchange. Tell him what you are looking for and ask for first refusal. Then get him chatting and tell him you'll write the name of his garage on the finished racer — half-an-hour later you ought to have him sponsoring the entire project.

Collectors' cars, as the motoring press chooses to call over-priced old tin, is an area best avoided. Things like Austin-Healey 3000s and Lotus Cortinas are best left to those with the cash. They're not really the style, anyway, and if I did buy an XK150 for pennies out in the sticks somewhere, I wouldn't drop in a Hemi and run it in Modified; I'd do it up, sell it and buy a new house with the proceeds.

Three marques — Alfa Romeo, Lancia and BMW — can be lumped together as junior league foreign exotica. They can all offer very fast cars which could drag very well indeed. All three makes lose their value very quickly indeed (not least because insurance is a real bitch) and bargains are easily found. The 2-litre Alfas, six-cylinder BMWs and 2-litre Lancias all

A blown Lotus engine stuffed into a tiny Berkeley body motivates Super Joker, the Cookson family's dinky Modified.

Kit cars make occasional appearances at the drags, and Alan Moore's TX Tripper is one of the more frequent visitors, running with 2-litre Vitesse power.

One of the really big killer Mopars, the Dodge Charger. Find one with the right engine and you're in business in a big way.

have single-figure 0-60 times, and in good condition can be found for under £1,000. The big problem is that they are expensive when they break, but if you are prepared to take that into account you could do very well.

Big league exoticars would not necessarily make good drag cars. Aston Martins, Ferraris and Porsches are jolly fast, but really geared for top-end performance rather than acceleration. AC and Lotus products would be better bets, but the whole range is far too expensive to consider here. I've always wanted to drag a Rolls-Royce, though, just for a giggle.

Going back in time, as they say, there are quite a few machines which were surprisingly fast, yet are frequently overlooked. Mini-Coopers are desperately unfashionable, but obviously rapid — but what about the 1750 HL Allegro? It ran 0-60 in 11.5 and that front-wheel drive would give good traction. They're difficult cars to work on, on the other hand, and would you be seen dead in one?

The other BMC/BLMC/Leyland/BL/Nuffield Motors possibility is the MGC, with the straight-six, or the MGB GT V8, with its Rover 3½-litre. Neither engine is the ideal dragging motor, but they'd be a fair start.

Other manufacturers, normally staid, have had their moments of glory. I've already mentioned the Sunbeam Tiger — the 289 V8-powered version of the Alpine — but Rootes/Chrysler were also responsible for a rapid version of the Avenger, confusingly called the Tiger Avenger — and the ugly but reasonably priced rapid H120 Sunbeam Rapier, with its Holbay Racing-prepared 110 bhp mill, with twin Webers and 9.6:1 compression. Then there was the Sunbeam Stiletto, a close cousin of the Hillman Imp Californian; twin carbs, high-lift cam, oil cooler — all that sort of stuff in a tiny 14-cwt car. The rear-engine, rear-wheel-drive set-up would be superb for traction, too.

As I said of the MGB GT V8, the Rover 3½ is not the best of dragging engines. It doesn't rev highly or freely enough, but it is a V8, has scope for improvement, and puts out 160 bhp in stock trim. The old 3.5-litre saloons and coupes weigh more than 31 cwt; forget them. But the Rover 3500, as the police used to use, only weighed 26 cwt, of which a lot could be jettisoned. They do 0-60 in 11 seconds and are jolly cheap nowadays. Possible; they'll not break in a hurry, and you could always sell the engine to a rodder for a goodly sum.

Triumph provides food for thought in the shape of the 2-litre Vitesse and the GT6. The GT6 is a Spitfire fitted with a fastback and Triumph's 2-litre six-pot; fair, with a 10-second 0-60 — but actually faster were the 2.5Pi saloons and estate cars. Lots of trim weight to be slung out, too. I'd go for the estate car for its better rear axle gearing — or perhaps change the gearing on a saloon. They look jolly boring, though, don't they? I'll come back to the Vitesse later.

Time to mention the Turbo Opel Manta, which would make a smashing racer. Not too expensive to buy, nowadays, but try finding one.

Vauxhall end the list of Surprisingly Rapid Quart Into Pint Pot Motors. Their SRQIPPM offerings revolve around two rather good engines; the 1.8-litre and the really good 110-bhp 2.3-litre. The bodyshells are the Magnum, Firenza and Ventora (both models). All very pretty and capable of 10-second 0-60s. They're not far off being ideal start machinery for either Street, Production, or bracket racing — and there's a good range of interchangeable diff ratios from things like Vivas, too. Any of them (except perhaps a droop-snoot Firenza) could be yours for around £800. Anyone for a 3.3-litre Ventora estate?

A number of late-model machines bear witness to the motor industry's rediscovery of the Quart Into Pint Pot formula. Unless you find one with repairable body damage or something, they'll still be expensive secondhand, but the machines to look for are the Renault Gordini, Ford Escort RS2000, or XR3, Talbot Lotus Sunbeam, Volkswagen Golf GTi, Volkswagen Sirocco GLi and Storm, and — a bizarre thought, but outrageously fast — Panther Lima Turbo. I've not seen any of these late cars on the strip yet (apart from on demo runs) but they could well be the shape of things to come.

Weight is a crucial factor in all drag cars, so if you are buying 'off the peg', it does make some sense to look for something which starts light and can then be lightened even further. Glass-fibre-bodied kit cars have their own appeal and their own fans; TVR, Marcos, Nova and the like form a small and specialized group. But what of the Bond Equipe and the Reliant Scimitar? Both can be obtained with good engine set-ups and are very light. The Scimitar — in both coupe and GTE versions — came equipped with either the 2.5 or 3-litre Ford V6, and weighed just over one ton. The most interesting Bond Equipe is the 2-litre GT; the 1,998-cc six-cylinder Triumph engine, putting out 104 bhp in an 18-cwt car. Very interesting, both.

American cars come in at the other end of the scale — invariably heavy and lugubrious. A complete book in themselves, I'm nervous of laying down the law on the subject. Because of engine improvements over the years, and the fashionable rise of street muscle in the Sixties, machinery of between 1964 and 1972 is favourite. American muscle cars and their engines have committed devotees who would argue every inch of the way for their particular marque; overall, though, the list which follows comprises desirable late-model Detroit muscle. It's not exclusive — allow for obscure exceptions, big-engined sedans and *my* prejudices.

Mopar: Introduced two of their best engines in '66, the 383 and the 426 Hemi, to be found in the Plymouth Belvedere and Satellite. Dodge Charger from '67 and the Coronet from the same year — with MoPar's third great engine, the 440 R/T (road and track). The GTX was a big hunky car, similar to the later Roadrunner. The Dart emerged with its 385 in '68, and was followed the next year by the Charger Daytona and Super Bee, while '69 was *the* year for the Roadrunner, as was '70 for the Superbird. Barracudas

This would always be my first choice for a street/strip slice of Detroit muscle, the beautiful, swoopy, '70-series Challenger.

The early fastback Mustang. The 289 is a reliable mill offering a lot of scope for improvement in easy stages.

85

were okay later and favourite with the 340. 1970 saw the introduction of what some would call the most beautiful, and last, muscle car; the Challenger. Put any of these cars together with any of the good engines (especially the 383, 440 or 426 Hemi) and you're in business.

Chevrolet: Corvettes and Camaros, really. Any year for the Vette, and the right engine (or the Z28 package) for the Camaro. All Vettes are good-to-beautiful, Camaros are fair-to-okay. For mills, start with the 327 and 350 small-blocks, and go up to the 396, 427 and 454 big blocks. Easy.

Pontiac: The Goat is second only to the Challenger as the bitchiest muscle machine — any year is a good year; from the 389 of 1966 to the 428. Firebirds; nice cars — watch out for 400, 455 and HO and Trans-Am packages.

Ford: The Mustang was born in '64, but forget straight-sixes. The 289 is small but certainly has its place, then it's 302, 351 (Cleveland better than Windsor) and the big blocks — 390, 427, 428 and Boss 429. Go for Shelby Mustangs, GT350s, GT500s and the Cobra Jet 428 mill, which also saw service in Ford XLs and some Mercurys. Mach Ones have their moments. Some Ford sedans, such as Galaxies, have good engines, but most are overweight family cars.

Oldsmobile: Machines like the 4-4-2 also serve. Engines are much as Pontiac (another GM subdivision). Avoid Toronado with its complex front-wheel drive.

American Motors: Javelin and AMX. Some folk like them, I don't.

Full engine details and weights and measurements of all the prominent American engines can be found in *The Complete Customiser,* which is published by Sphere and written by Steven Myatt (plug).

Back home. Were I starting from scratch, going out to buy a car which I would either run in Production with its standard mill, or in Street with the engine modified, there are three machines which I would recommend.

Firstly: The 2-litre Triumph Vitesse Mk 2. The bodyshell was designed for the Herald range and was originally powered by the 39-bhp 1,147 engine. The 2-litre Vitesse weighed an extra two hundredweight, but could lay claim to 104 bhp from its twin-Stromberg-aspirated mill. The one-piece flip front gives excellent access and the independent transverse-leaf rear suspension gets it off the line quite cleanly. The gearbox is good, and fast in operation, though it doesn't have synchromesh on first. A straight-forward project to turn into a Production or bracket car, and I'd look to a 2.5 motor (either injected or with triple Webers) from one of the big saloons to take it up a notch or two to Modified later on. A large range of rear gearing ratios is available from Heralds and estate car variations.

Secondly: A 3-litre V6 Capri. Ford's V6 is a smashing engine. In its Mk 1 Capri GT form, it produces 140 bhp in a car weighing just over one ton and it's strong and versatile. Ford's gearboxes have well-spaced cogs; a Capri 3-litre will cover the quarter-mile in a respectable 16 (0-60, 8.5 seconds), using only first and second should you wish. You can go at the whole Ford range if you want to change the back axle. The V6 is getting very popular, and a fair amount of speed equipment — from replacement carbs and cams right up to bolt-on superchargers — is now readily available. A good early Capri can cost you less than £750 — twice the price of a Vitesse Mk 2, incidentally, but you've probably got more to work on from there onwards.

Thirdly: Jaguar XJ12. Over the past year or so these have become fabulous value for money. They are expensive to run on the road from most respects and their prices have plummetted. £500 would get you one, and if you don't happen across an XJ12, then a 4.2 XJ6 couldn't be far behind. The engines on the 12s are complex — especially when fitted with fuel-injection, but if you feel up to that then you can look to seeing off V8s with ease; 285 bhp has got to be a good start, and you can lose a lot of the stock 38 cwt. Axle ratios are all interchangeable with the 2.8, 3.4 and 4.2 six-cylinder cars. A well-sorted XJ12 running in Production could easily run 14s; I'm just surprised it hasn't been done. Anybody got an XJ12 coupe they don't want?

BUILDING A BRACKET BOMBER/ STREET CLASS CAR

To write a section about how to build a competitive drag car I've got to make a lot of basic assumptions. Obviously I'm not about to tell you how to build a Funny Car in five easy steps, but following on from what we've already seen, it is possible to point out the criteria for building an effective racer which remains street legal, and would either run healthily in the brackets or in Street or Production in class racing. So, this section of the book can only really be seen as a set of broad-based guidelines which can be applied where relevant.

My first assumption, especially after the last chapter, is that you have your car. There are now half a dozen or so separate areas which need to come under close scrutiny, and though you may approach them in whatever order suits you, I shall deal first with bodywork and lightening.

As I say, the intention is to keep the car street legal (so that you don't restrict yourself from class racing), but if you intend to concentrate on bracket bombing alone then there will be a few points you can take even further. Mind you, I do suspect that once you start letting go of street-legality you'll be more than a touch inclined to go the whole hog and start radical operations which may only leave you with Comp Altered. It is also worth pointing out at this stage that unless you are both clever and conscientious, you're possibly heading (metaphorically) down a one-way street. Your car will have a resale value as a racer, but not as a street car. Yes, it is a point to bear in mind. Putting everything back to stock could well be impossible, or at the best uneconomical. Hedging your bets and keeping the car 'stock-ish' so that you preserve its 'straight' resale value is a matter of compromise. The choice is yours and all you have to do is apply some commonsense.

Bodywork

A car's performance output is governed by many factors, but ultimately it comes down to power-to-weight ratio. Putting it very crudely, drop the same engine and drive train into a 1-ton car and a 2-ton car and the former will go more quickly (don't worry, we'll get to the finer details soon). Look up the weight of your car in the handbook — or even take it to a weighbridge — and make a note of that figure. A Mk 1 Capri 3-litre weighs 21¼ cwt, a '69 351 Boss Mustang 25½ cwt and an XJ6 32½ cwt... better though to think in pounds (lb) as an English hundredweight (at 112 lb) is different from an American hundredweight (a more logical 100 lb). So make that 2,380 lb, 2,856 lb, and 3,640 lb, respectively.

The Capri's GT 3-litre, as we've seen, produces 140 bhp; and with that power-to-weight ratio manages low 16-second quarters. As 140 bhp hauling 2,380 lb equals (say) 16.2 seconds, obviously 140 bhp pulling 2,000 lb is going to equal a figure well below 16. Given all the information I could draw you a very convincing graph.

The process is not without its drawbacks, however. The car's basic strength must be retained, and in places additional strengthening may have

An ultra-light aluminium panel fits into the footwell of the 100E. It was made up by cutting and shutting a cardboard template first, then it only needed trimming and filing.

to be inserted where weight-shedding operations have left a real or potential weakness. Also, a car can be *too* light, and one enters the worrying equations of weight distribution and loss of traction. Weight distribution is not immediately pertinent, though, and traction comes later, so let's be more positive just for a moment.

With a tendency to overlook the obvious, many folk spend a lot of time and a lot more money making their engine produce more power, rather than persuading it to produce the right sort of power or ensuring that the power already available is put to the best use. Body lightening makes the available power do more work and, in the main, is very cheap.

The interior is as good a place as anywhere. Take out the seats and all the trim panels, as well as the window-winding mechanisms and the carpets, and you'll find that the scruffy pile on your front lawn adds up to about 150 lb on a Capri and more than twice that on the XJ6. This isn't a total saving, of course, as you've got to put something back in its place. According to your class you might be able to dispense with all but the driver's seat — and that can be replaced with a lighter item (bought from a race supplier, pirated

The back of the 100E before carpeting was little more than an expanse of aluminium. The wheelarches are original steel, though, for simplicity's sake.

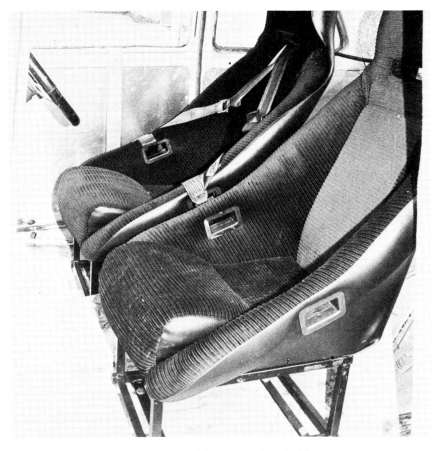

We located the new lightweight racing seats early on and, using heavy body washers beneath, bolted them down so that when we were ready to add the lightweight carpet we were able to bolt this in place and, working outwards, trim and fit the edges.

from a scrapyard, or even your old seat cut down). The interior on Dennis' 100E shows the route he took — all the trim panels were replaced with pop-riveted aluminium sheeting (as light as you'll get and easily fabricated). Wherever possible we backed the ally with a thin variety of the sort of asbestos padding used to insulate lofts — and that's a great help in eliminating the sort of booming resonance that can build up. The firewall is double-skinned aluminium stuffed solid with asbestos.

The replacement carpet is of a thin and lightweight type which is readily available and none too expensive (about £5 per yard off a 66-inch wide roll). All the window-winding mechanisms have been junked and replaced by a

Aluminium replaces the door panel trim and lengths of old seat belt are used for door stops and, railway carriage-style, window operation.

studded strap. We could have gone a step further and installed Perspex side windows, another considerable weight-saving, but we want to keep the car totally street legal. Perspex is not on for road use.

The fastidious will then turn their attention to the dashboard and its ancillaries. Standard steering wheels can weigh 12 lb — can you afford a lighter racing one? Don't go cutting up the old one, though. Can you cut down the dash or replace it with covered ally? And do you really need that bulky centre console, pretty though it might look? Once you start looking you'll be surprised by how many frilly and purely cosmetic bits and pieces you find. At this stage the truly dedicated will either throw away their heater and all its hoses and controls and replace it with a smaller, lighter unit (worth a visit to a scrapyard), or either do without, or get a little plug-in 12-volt unit. Replacing necessary ancillaries such as the washers and wiping systems is usually more trouble than its worth, but have a peek at it anyway.

Outside, there'll be a lot of obvious scope. Badges and styling follies can go the way of the bumpers and their irons — though it may ease your mind to sort some small nudge bars to keep the careless at bay. On a large car, and especially on an American car, the weight of the bumpers alone will surprise you — the total weight of all extraneous exterior fittings could total 150 lb.

The main structure of the car should be left well alone — especially on cars of monocoque construction — where strength is created by integral panel components. I do know owners of big American muscle cars who have had major panels such as wings and doors acid-dipped to reduce their thickness and hence their weight, but I'd think it more trouble than it is really worth, and certainly a job which I would only trust to a real specialist.

Items which can be replaced more easily are the bonnet and boot. Glass-fibre replicas will weigh about a third of the originals. You'll not be able to mount them to the original hinges, though, and the best approach is to fabricate tabs with quick-release fasteners so that each panel can be quickly undone and then completely removed from the car. Handy for access, too. The only real danger with glass-fibre bonnets and boots is that folk tend to lean on them — especially when they're about to tell you something particularly boring — and 14-stone of gossiping racer can be disastrous.

There are proprietory glass-fibre panels available over the counter for a number of cars — from Ford Pops to '55 Chevies — and these can include wings and complete one-piece flip-fronts where the grille, the bonnet and the wings are formed as a single unit. Flip-fronts are a boon for working on the engine, and can either be front-hinged to arc forward, or be totally detachable. In virtually every case, though (the exceptions being things like E-types and Triumph Heralds, where flip-fronts came as standard) the wings and inner wings are load-bearing components and stout reinforcing will have to be substituted.

Weight-shedding under the bonnet is generally minimal and retaining strength here is all-important. Inner wings can be removed, but should almost certainly be replaced by struts. Peppering any flat or L-section struts (drilling holes along it so that the actual mass of metal is reduced by between a third and a half) can be dangerous, and should be done sparingly.

Radiators can be swopped for smaller units, but the weight-saving is rarely large and must be considered against any danger of over-heating; Bracket cars don't always get long cool-off periods between races.

A major job up the sharp end which could lose a considerable amount of weight, especially — again — on American cars, is to replace the front suspension with a simple tube axle. Twin longitudinal leaves on a chromed tube axle will not only weigh a lot less than the usual American set-up of hefty coils on huge semi-wishbones, but also look terrific and give the car a high stance which, along with race suspension, will improve weight transfer on take-off. It will also make cornering a bit of a bitch, but what you lose on the street you gain on the strip.

The boot is one area where it doesn't always pay to shed too much weight. Weight over the rear axle is advantageous (see later), but the one thing to look at is the fuel tank. The 100E was a typical application. Fuel tanks tend to be either mounted to one side or slung under the boot floor some way

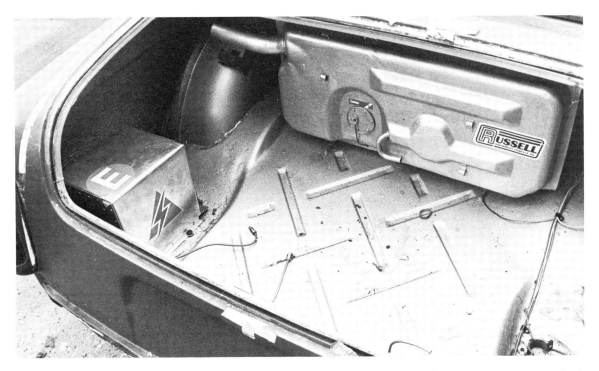

back from the axle. The new tank on the 100E is smaller and lighter and now mounts directly and centrally over the axle area, solidly mounted above and below, and insulated from the rear bulkhead with the ubiquitous asbestos. I seem to remember Dennis and I pirating the tank from an Austin Cambridge in a scrapyard near Warrington; it looked the right sort of size and shape.

As well as being a series of specific jobs, keeping the car's weight down is a thought to have in the back of your mind throughout the rest of the build-up. Don't go adding weight unnecessarily as you become infatuated with the goodies on display in your local speed shop, and with ancillaries you will find that it is possible to get lighter-than-stock items — batteries, for example. I have trouble even lifting the huge battery fitted to my old Jaguar, and though one of that size is essential for a road car with that engine capacity and those electrical accessories, you would not need one so large for a day's racing. Find yourself a small battery in good condition and keep it well charged-up and it'll easily fire the motor as often as needed on the day. (We always carry jump-leads and a spare battery when we remember it.)

Weight-transfer

An obvious follow-on; having taken the weight of your racer down as far as possible, that bulk must now be put to best effect. The basic principle is simple and vitally important. The vast majority of race cars are front-engined coupled to rear-wheel drive, and on take-off as much as possible of the car's weight must stress through the car from front to back to ensure that the rear wheels dig in as efficiently as possible. On a circuit car or even a dragster it is important to have the lowest possible centre of gravity — for superior cornering in the first case, and to maintain its aerodynamics and keep it on the strip in the second case. With bracket cars and Street, Production, and Modified classes, it's a distinct advantage for the car to sit slightly higher so that the centre of gravity is correspondingly higher and there is greater capacity for weight-transfer.

This phrase — weight-transfer — can be a bit worrying. Nothing within the car actually moves relative to anything else, but if you can recall anything from your school physics lessons, the notions of thrust and dynamics might ring a bell. Dynamics is a branch of the scientific definition of 'mechanics' — which is the study of the action of forces on bodies in motion. Don't panic, it's not that bad. For our purpose, the dynamic reaction of weight-transfer which takes place when a car launches from the line is — physically — that the front of the car lifts away from the wheels (though, ideally, the front wheels do not leave the ground) and the car's weight pushes back through the car, squats the rear suspension, and forces its impetus down on to the driving wheels.

A few yards from the line you then want the front end to be coming back slowly, so that your aerodynamics improve as your speed increases. We need to move on to a new sub-heading to explain how all this can be achieved. Have you, though, ever seen those jokey little cartoons of cars curving in the middle, their noses in the air, as they launch from a start-line? Well there's a lot more scientific truth in that than you might previously have thought.

Suspension

Starting at the front, what is needed here is a set-up which allows this process we've just been talking about — a system where the front end comes up steeply on take-off and then goes down steadily and none too quickly. The answer is straightforward and lies with the shock absorbers. A small number of specialist speed shops will be able to set you up with what are known as 90/10 shock absorbers. This figure denotes percentages of downwards and upwards resistance within the unit. A shock absorber is a piston compressing fluid to induce internal resistance and according to its construction can extend more easily than it contracts. This is the case with 90/10s — 90% of their capacity is resistance to the downwards movement, and 10% is the percentage of resistance to upwards movement. So, as you launch they happily open out and let the front of your car come right up, then they take their time letting the weight settle.

These 90/10s are impractical and illegal for street use, however, so you'll need to be able to swap them with a conventional set. Some cheap racers simply run on very old and worn front shockers; these allow the front of the car to do its lifting bit alright, but haven't the resistance to let it down gradually.

If your front suspension set-up includes coil springs (not coils over shocks, though), it is possible to fit small air-bags within the spring itself. These can be inflated with a conventional pump for racing and then deflated to bring the nose down for road use. The American race parts catalogue also include front-lift kits for American cars (for race use only) which either space out the ball-joints or lift the coil springs away from the A-frame. These lift the nose right enough, but obviously have no provision to allow it to drop again and steering at the top end can be adversely affected.

Rear suspension needs to be firm and must be able to cope with two problems. The first of these will come under the general heading of 'traction' and relates as much to the axle itself as to the suspension; we'll come to that shortly. What the rear suspension must be set up to handle is 'pre-load'. Have you ever watched a car burnout and noticed that the smoke was rising from only one wheel? Or that on leaving the line it left only one tyre mark? Axles are not symmetrical, and the engine's power comes along the car in a circular motion. Think about it. With an imbalance of torque one wheel is working harder than the other and the car pitches diagonally.

There are various ways of getting round this problem; either pre-load weight or use height-adjustment. The crudest method is to hike up the back by fitting extended spring shackles and having the right-hand side higher than the left — a similar method (still on a leaf-sprung car) is to have one or even two more leaves on the right-hand side. A couple of solutions which offer more precise adjustment are to either have air-bags in the springs (as at the front) on a coil-and-shocks set-up and inflate the right-hand side more than the left until balance is achieved, or to fit air shocks. These are like conventional shock absorbers, but their resistance can be increased or decreased by pumping compressed air, and unequal pressures will obviously have the desired effect.

The weight-distribution approach looks rather different. For a start, if you've got to have weight in the boot it may well help to have it over the left-hand side, but some racers refine the approach much further by installing a slotted transverse bar along which a bracket can be moved. The bracket can be loaded with weight-training bar-bells of the optimum total weight and adjusted until the best loading is achieved. There again, some people just experiment with their slick pressures.

Traction

This is an extension of the rear axle/suspension set-up, and just about the most important area for an ambitious racer to attend to. We're back with that notion of ensuring that you make the best possible use of all the

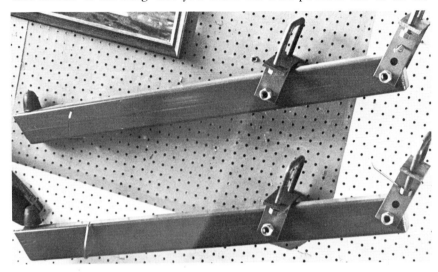

Looking tempting on the speed shop wall, a pair of anti-tramp style traction bars.....

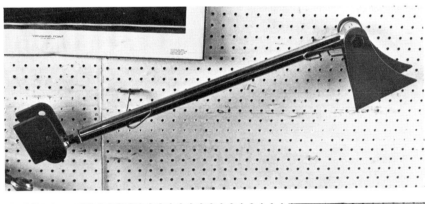
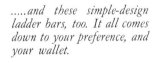

.....and simple bolt-up traction bars.....

.....and these simple-design ladder bars, too. It all comes down to your preference, and your wallet.

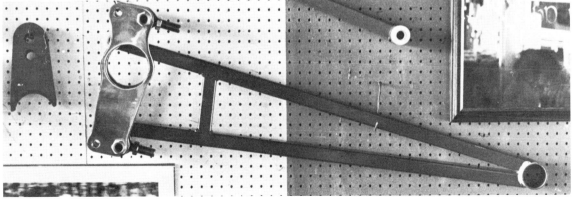

available power and torque. (Torque is an expression of power-created thrust and is rated in lbs/ft.) Under hard acceleration rear tyres tend to do all sorts of useless things — hopping around, bouncing about, and generally doing anything but digging in and getting you away from the line. Tramping, that's the word.

The rear axle doesn't really want to be doing quite what you've got in mind. All that power comes down the prop-shaft, turns through two 90-degree angles and wants to start 'winding up' the axle. Conventional suspension systems let it do so (for the sake of a comfortable ride) and the axle moves the wheels up and down, and backwards and forwards, relative to the car itself. The trick is to get some larger degree of solidity between the axle and car to limit the axle's lateral travel.

Independent rear suspension (IRS) is by no means unknown on British drag racers. Corvettes come with stock IRS, of course, and ex-Jaguar IRSs find their way on to all sorts of machines. Tramping on any IRS is easily cured by a simple bolt-up traction bar. This is a length of square-section tube with a swivel-jointed plate at each end. One either side, mounting the base of the suspension to the chassis, ensures that the suspension can move up and down, but not backwards or forwards.

Solid axles are either located by leaf springs and shocks, or by coils and shocks. The usual traction bar application for leaf springs consists of a square-section tube which either locates to the U-bolt base plate or is clamped to the leaf on either side of the base, and stretches forward so that under acceleration the rubber stop at the front end makes contact with the twisting leaf spring and flattens it out. This style of traction bar needs some precise setting up (it should end beneath the spring eye and sit about one inch below it); is not completely effective, and can bend away under pressure in some cases. I've seen IRS-style bolt-up traction bars available for leaf-sprung cars in the speed shops that would be as effective.

I don't have too high a regard for 'pinion snubbers' which are hard rubber snubbers (like suspension bump stops) mounted on brackets which attach to the front of the diff and bang up against a reinforced plate on the chassis when the axle tries to curve under heavy torque.

Best of all are ladder bars. These are triangular frames with cross-braces which fit to the axle and taper forward to a spherical rod end which bolts to the chassis. As an axle tries to wind up under the torque of acceleration, the impetus is transferred along the bottom member of the ladder base, and then dissipates — up at an angle into the chassis, but also back along the upper bar — and forces the front of the car up, helping to press the axle back down. The force on a bolt-up anti-tramp bar, on the other hand, simply goes straight forward through the front mount, while on a snubber it goes vertically into the chassis.

At this point it's worth mentioning wheelie bars. These are small wheels

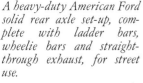

A heavy-duty American Ford solid rear axle set-up, complete with ladder bars, wheelie bars and straight-through exhaust, for street use.

on triangular struts which stretch back from the axle. Should the car's front wheels lift right off the ground the wheelie bars should limit how far it goes ('should' — because they've got to take a lot of strain). There are wheelie bars available which are part of a ladder-bar system; these just don't absorb the shock of a wheelie, but feed the force back into the suspension to help bring the car back down.

Rear axles and ratios

From your rear axle you want two things — strength, and the optimum gearing ratio for the final-drive.

A very common source of sudden drag defeat is to lose by default with rear-end failure. I can recall occasions when I've sat with the engine blatting happily and the car going nowhere at all for want of a half-shaft or diff gearing.

So, you need a rear axle which was designed to take the power which your car is producing, and, if you *are* swopping axles, find one of the same width — unless you are prepared to take the housing and half-shafts to be shortened by a specialist (and it must be a specialist!)

Going back to our Capri and/or XJ, I would be entirely confident of the strength of either's back axle, assuming we were going for a moderate power increase (and when we get to engines you'll see that strength, dependability and mild tuning work are preferable to taking the mill itself to the limit). As a generalization, if you don't change the engine, you needn't change the axle. If I were putting a mild V8 in the Capri I'd probably look to a solid Mk 2 Jag axle (less fuss than an IRS, but that's a personal preference), and if I were taking it further I'd pass over van axles and head for something which once lived under the back of some Detroit muscle. There are no set rules — just the guideline of using an axle originally intended to handle the horsepower your car is now putting out, and this is one occasion when you're allowed to exaggerate the BHP rating.

Diffs, really, are self-explanatory once you start stripping them down. The power comes down through the prop-shaft, which turns the pinion, which then turns the crownwheel, which is held in place ultimately by two sets of bearings. The half-shafts are splined and slot in on either side to then turn the road wheels.

A dirty weekend spent checking the axle is certainly a good idea. Look at the prop-shaft UJs (up-rated ones are available for most Yank cars), replace them if in doubt, and then check the splines on the half-shafts and the teeth on the diff crownwheel and pinion. As you are putting it back together, replace the bearings, just in case.

The relationship between the pinion and crownwheel is the 'diff ratio' — the number of times the pinion has to turn before the crownwheel completes one revolution. By changing the diff ratio (swopping the pinion and crownwheel on many interchangeable axles) a car can be geared for either better acceleration or an improved top end. In stock condition the ratio is a compromise, so there is usually something to be gained; but take it too far and you'll launch in a scream of revs, have to change up within a second or two, and will have run out of steam half-way up the strip. To increase take-off rather than top-end, you need to change the diff for one which is numerically higher . . . the stock final-drive ratio on the 3-litre V6 Capri is 3.090:1, and that's interchangeable with the V4 Capri's 3.222:1, or the 1.6 or 1.3's 3.444:1 — so that's the way to be going. Beyond that I'd be looking to change the axle for one from the Zephyr/Zodiac/Consul range, which could offer ratios of 3.9:1 on a V6 Zodiac, right up to 4.625:1 on a Mk 1 Consul.

The other variable is the size of your rear wheels and tyres. Increasing wheel size from, say, the standard 13-inch diameter of a Capri to 14s will have the effect of numerically lowering your ratio and slowing your take-off ability. But you can compensate for that with a diff-ratio change . . . aaaargh.

One of the American magazines once gave me a little cardboard calculator which equated horsepower and overall weight, to give the car's ECW and project its ET and terminal speed, while on the other side, one of the permutations allowed you to equate final-drive ratio against maximum engine revs and maximum tyre diameter, to find the car's top speed. On the first of those calculations two things worry me; that American horsepower and BHP aren't immediately comparable, and that their estimation of terminal speed tends to the high side. (A more conservative chart is used on occasion at drag strips in this country to calculate a terminal speed where only an ET has been recorded.)

Given that the 2,380-lb/138-bhp Capri can run 16/86 (with an ECW of 19 lb/ci), taking the weight down to 2,000 lb and the bhp up to 200 should reduce the ECW to 10.3 and give times of 13/105.

There are mathematical equations behind all this, and they're going to make your brain ache. It's almost impossible to accurately compute a quarter-mile time, but you can work out your car's top speed and then bring that down on a sliding scale.

You need to know how many times your rear wheel goes round to cover one mile; the circumference of the Capri's tyre is 72 inches — exactly 6 feet. So if we divide the number of feet in a mile (5,280) by 6, we find that the wheel rotates 880 times per mile.

Top speed equals maximum engine revs divided by the final-drive ratio, then divided by the wheel rotations per mile, times 60 (for minutes per hour). Allowing the 3-litre to rev to a modest 5,500 revs and dividing that by its 3.09:1 stock diff ratio (call it a straight 3), we get 1,833 which, when further divided by the rotations per mile of 880, gives just under 21. Multiply that by 60 and we get a theoretical top speed of 126 mph — which sounds about right to me.

Once you've done that equation for the car in stock condition and have the top speed as a constant, you can start altering the formation of the equation to introduce variables. For example, final-drive ratio equals maximum revs multiplied by 60, divided by top speed, times wheel rotation. With that equation you can alter the tyre size to allow for bigger wheels, or assume an increase in engine revving ability, and see what diff ratio would bring you back to stock performance, And, of course, in the first formula you can alter the diff ratio to see what effect that would have. Having done all the maths, I can tell you that changing the Capri's axle for the Mk 1 Consul item with the 4.625:1 diff mentioned above, and keeping the stock rear wheels, would give you a maximum speed of 72 mph. Adding 15-inch rear wheels with a circumference of 9 ft to this Consul-diffed Capri brings that top speed back up to 110 mph.

All of which may well be making life far more complex than necessary for you and your potential bracket bomber. If your rear axle is strong and your engine modifications are mild, don't worry about the diff until you need to. Run the car, see how it feels, and then consider swopping ratios.

Transmission

Manual or auto? That's the question. By and large, a manually-shifted gearbox will always be quicker — or rather, allow you a slightly lower ET — but an automatic will be more consistent. It is generally considered that a manual box is better and more flexible for class racing, while an auto is a great help in bracket racing. If, though, your car is currently equipped with a good manual box and you want to take it bracket racing (or vice versa), fair enough.

The important factor in either set-up is strength and reliability. In any class of race car the transmission takes a lot of kicking around, but when actually rolling no more than in regular use. The real strain on any transmission is the initial impact of the launch, and if anything is going to break that's probably when and where it will happen.

Manual gearboxes first. If your stock box is in good condition and not already making any dread noises on shifting gear, you are almost certainly alright. Some boxes are obviously better than others — some Ford cars, for example, came with close-ratio boxes which can be a boon for dragging — but for the moment we will assume its performance and concentrate on the physical operation of the thing, and there are two factors in that — the clutch and the shifter.

The clutch is a door between engine and gearbox; it can be opened to

Specially designed and constructed clutch plates are available and are almost inevitably American-made. These are stronger and dissipate heat more efficiently.

allow the engine's revs through the box and hence to the back wheels, or closed to either allow gear shifting or the anticipation of shifting. The clutch, simply, comprises abrasive-coated free-spinning discs which function by friction when pressed together to let the revs through, or can be levered apart and kept under spring pressure when disengaged. The clutch is the crucial component in your transmission — its action must be smooth and gradual as the torque comes bounding through, yet operate quickly and with the maximum pedal control.

Assuming our ubiquitous 3-litre Capri to be a few years old, I would want to take the clutch apart and renew everything in sight — plates, springs and release bearings. Well worth checking with a speed shop or your local brand-dealer to see if uprated components are available for your model. Ferodo, at beautiful Chapel-en-le-Frith, make up racing clutches to special order. There are two things you are looking to improve by the use of non-stock parts; firstly, longevity — a tougher set-up is less likely to give way with a bang as you leave the line — and, yes, that is a danger. Secondly, you want better heat dissipation. All that torque going through the clutch is energy (energy which cannot be created or destroyed — where do you remember that from?) and under stress will convert itself into heat, which destroys the fabric of the plates, causing wear, and sometimes sudden wear. Competition clutch plates are faced with metallic rather than 'organic' materials, which can cope with much higher temperatures. Competition plates are also ventilated, as some disc brakes are, for improved heat dissipation. Competition pressure plates are available from speed shops, as are complete comp clutch units, and special lightening and ventilated flywheels, but they are hardly necessary for the standard of racing we're looking at.

Higher up the dragging scale, on fuellers and the like, you start moving into Crowerglide and 'slider' clutches, the first operating by centrifugal

Position the new shifter carefully so that it falls just to hand and is not going to snag the seats.

force alone, and 'sliders' being specially designed to absorb some of the initial torque and actually slip at first but then feed the power through as the car progresses. Needless to say, you should also check the hydraulic operations; new fluid and seals won't take you long.

Shifters. Slang expression referring to gear-changing devices. A good shifter is vital for dragging — you've got to be able to shift gear as quickly and cleanly as possible. Column-mounted shifters are virtually useless, and many stock floor shifts have levers far too long, leading to wasted effort on your part as your energy is absorbed by the lever, and having to aim the lever across too great a distance is all too imprecise. A specialist imported American race shifter gives much better control over the cogs, and once you've tried a drag shift you'll appreciate its speed and precision. A further refinement is a more positive reverse gate, so that the chances of accidentally hitting reverse gear are greatly reduced. Performance shifters start from around £60 and are a good investment.

Automatic transmission. Well, for a start, what I've just said applies equally to auto transmission shifting; go through the speed shop's range and choose the one that feels right for your palm — rod or cable-shifted as appropriate. Once installed you'll find you can shift much quicker and with much greater confidence. And if it's cable-operated keep a close watch on its condition.

Auto boxes in themselves instill fear and loathing in many people, and are simply tins of mystery. The core of an auto box is the torque converter. This bolts to the flywheel and is faced with fins on the inside. These press the transmission fluid hard against a central stator, which is allowed to rotate in one direction, and directs the fluid at low revs when it is being held stationary. As the revs increase and the speed of the torque convertor rises above the 'stall speed', the stator begins spinning until its speed equals that of the rest of the unit, thus setting up a turbine effect between the fins. The pressure of the fluid itself passing a series of valves within a separate block causes the gears to engage and disengage.

This 'stall speed' business is important. It is the point at which the unit starts to become operational. This can be established if you don't have the written information anywhere, by holding the car on both foot and hand brakes and, with the shifter in 'drive', pressing the accelerator down until the revs will rise no further. (Take it very easy with this test — do it quickly and infrequently.) For racing purposes a higher stall speed than stock is useful; specialists can supply high-stall-speed torque converters, and dual-speed converters which offer varied stall speeds at the touch of a button have recently become available over here.

Auto boxes are commonly supposed to be weaker and in some ways more temperamental than manual gearboxes, but so long as their working capacity is not exceeded and they are regularly serviced they are entirely adequate for drag use.

The first clue to basic service lies with the transmission fluid. Heavy use of an auto trans — like a manual — produces heat, and this will break up the molecular structure of the fluid. If it smells burned or dark brown in colour, replace it. On any car the auto fluid should be changed at least once a year. As with an oil change on an engine, always change the filter. The auto trans filter is located inside the trans sump. Never over-fill or under-fill with fluid, either; the former will cause sluggish movement, and the latter will result in overheating and fluid foaming or being forced out of the unit and the upwards movement of the gears will also slow down.

Engine vacuum lines (where fitted) must be checked, as must the shift operation. Some kick-downs are operated via an electrical connection from the throttle — check the connections and even the fuse.

I would not advise the inexperienced to investigate or overhaul their own automatic transmission. Leave it to the experts, who can uprate the trans to competition standards while they are about it. But the slusher is certainly nothing to be frightened of, and its consistency will be a great help in the bracket pairings.

Wheels and slicks

The first thing you notice about a slick is that it hasn't got a tread. Yes? No. The tread is the surface of the tyre which makes contact with the ground . . . so a slick, unlike a road tyre, hasn't got a *patterned* cut tread. Right. Now, why not? The purpose of a patterned tread is to disperse water. Slicks are designed, European weather withstanding, for use in the dry alone.

The purpose of a slick is to gain maximum grip and thereby minimize the wheelspin which a patterned tyre would allow (think about it — a patterned tyre only has a proportion of its surface on the road at any one time). The slick's job is to harness the maximum amount of the car's power to induce forward velocity by joining the tyre and the ground as efficiently as possible so that all the power goes down in one spot.

So how does it do it? There are three main factors. Firstly, the slick is made of a very soft rubber compound so that it gets very hot very quickly in the burnout, and virtually 'glues' itself to the strip. During the burnout, and as they launch the car from the line, the slicks alter in shape with the heat —

This dramatic shot of Dennis Priddle's old Mister Six rear-seater shows how far the slick grows and how tall it becomes in those first vital seconds.

they grow taller and thinner and the pressure inside increases dramatically so that the impetus is being pressed through a smaller and tighter area of rubber (a stiletto heel comes down with a greater lbs/psi force than does the heel of one of your brothel creepers). Secondly, and related to that last point, the slick's construction is such that it allows all this to take place. The sidewalls are of a different form than the tread. They need not, indeed, even be rubber, but are generally a flimsy 2-ply (as opposed to 4-ply) so that they wrinkle when the car is at rest, but can physically stretch when under pressure. A very pronounced 'wrinkle-wall' effect is gained on some cars by fitting oversize slicks to wheels which are smaller than the recommended width, and the slick overhangs. Not a good idea for smaller machinery, though; too much stickiness means too great an initial resistance and you'll only shatter your half-shafts. The process of raising and narrowing, as mentioned above, also has an obvious effect on the car's final gearing — effectively shifting it as the machine is in motion. For larger cars running big slicks this can be a crucial factor.

The slick's rubber compound content varies, with heavier cars running on harder compounds. Slicks, then, are not always interchangeable — though the drivers of some relatively heavy Production and Modified cars have been experimenting successfully with slicks designed for much lighter Comp Altereds. The problem with that is that it halves the slicks' life which, on a Production car, should be up to three years, depending on how hard you burnout. Sylvia and Geoff Hauser, running 14-inch wide slicks, are going through three pairs of slicks a season thanks to Sylvia's big burnouts. At around £90-£120 per slick!

There are no speed ratings for slicks as there are for road tyres, but your supplier will calculate size against revs and speed to provide you with the correct size of slick for your car. Pressures vary with the car's weight, but 8 to 10 lbs/psi on a Production car would be about right. The trick is to draw a few chalk marks across the slick and see how evenly it gets rubbed off during a burnout. If only the edges go then your pressures are too low, and if the centre of the line is rubbed off the pressures are too high.

All slicks have inner tubes. Slicks fitted to cars capable of more than 150 mph may also have safety liners — an inner tyre which holds the car upright and keeps the tyre firm in the event of serious slick damage.

To some degree, in the States especially, slicks have outgrown their

Slim M&H front drag tyres on very light alloy American Racing Equipment wheels, a set-up intended for the upper dragging classes. The narrowness means less air resistance.

wheels in terms of both physical size and technology. Driving wheels need to be both as light and as strong as possible. Steel and banded steel come bottom of the list, with the better slot-mag wheels nearing the top. The best wheel for the job is the purpose-built smooth alloy-faced American dragging wheel. Split rim or no depends on your use. They cost money but are the best. On balance, though, if you haven't got a piggy bank large enough to cope with both wheels and slicks from the top of the range I would recommend spending the money on the slicks and having them wrapped round a set of the better custom alloy wheels — which can often be found secondhand in the classified ads of the custom magazines. Some people who cannot even afford a pair of drag slicks try running on very worn street tyres — hardly a good idea as they are of a completely different structure and are liable to blow — or they try old circuit-racing slicks, which are better than nothing, but tend to be too hard, especially on the walls.

Engine work

Assumption time again. I'm assuming that we're still working on a budget and are aiming at Street and/or the brackets. So I am further going to assume that you're not about to strip and rebuild your engine just for dragging. I assume a strong and reliable mill which will accept minor ancillary modifications. To try and write here about camshaft profiles and strengthened bearings would be wrong; the subject needs a whole book, and the applications are too varied for generalizations — when building for dragging one requires different things from different sizes and styles of engine.

There are areas of common ground, though; ignition, exhaust systems, basic maintenance and the like are what we'll look at.

The one generalization I can make is to say that first and foremost — even above increasing power output — a drag car's engine needs to be strong, reliable and consistent. Given a basic and well-built motor in good condition, headers and carb changes, etc, will make it much more efficient, and that gain — coupled with toughness and the all-important word consistency — will add up to a competitive Street or bracket car. Compression alterations, a tough bottom-end, a hotter cam, and balanced pistons and rods are all mods to look to when you decide that you really want to go faster and a total rework is in order. Run more slowly and teach yourself to be a good drag racer first.

Vital Fluids/1: Petrol

As you will see when we get on to carburation, petrol vapour supply to the engine is no hit-or-miss affair; so also with the supply of the petrol itself. It would be of no use asking the system to supply more if it simply wasn't possible. Check the petrol pipe from the tank to the pump and replace with race-standard plumbing where necessary — bend it as little as possible, keep it away from heat, avoid restrictive fittings, and make sure of all joins. Even more importantly, check out the capacity of the petrol pump itself, good racing pressure would be around 6 psi. This is something to be done with the expert down at the speed shop — a good one who'll pause for a moment to give proper advice rather than just keep on taking notes out of your hand. Always go for an electrical rather than a mechanical pump as it will deliver at a constant pressure and not flutuate with the revs. Cost of a good 'un? About £30. There should be no problem in relating the pump and the pump-to-carb(s) pipe to the size of your improved carburation. A fuel filter is a good idea, but must be fitted between the pump and the carb(s).

Vital Fluids/2: Oil

Oil pump failure is not an uncommon cause of grenaded engines. New oil and a new filter (never use an old one) from the start of your dragging career goes without saying. If you can remove the sump and drain off the gunge, all the better. Magnetizing the end of the dipstick, so that any metallic jetsam is held and then removed every time you inspect the level, is a neat idea.

The standard oil pump should be up to the task of racing, but it might be a smart move to fit a higher relief valve. This will allow the oil pressure to rise; a standard 40 psi could go up to 60. All that's needed is a change of spring, and while the advantage is improved lubrication, the only disadvantage is increased oil wear. Yes, oil does wear out — and on a street/strip car should be changed every 1,000 miles.

An oil cooler, should you feel you need one, will cost you around £35. On a spin-on filter set-up it will plumb into an adaptor plate, while it can be easily installed in-line with a remote filter. Some people try using old heater radiators for this task — don't; they're not up to the high pressure the thing will have to stand.

Vital Fluids/3: Water

Apart from rinsing and back-flushing the cooling system (washing it under high pressure in the opposite direction to its normal flow), all you want your water to do for you is to allow the engine to operate at its optimum temperature. Check for leaks, as in all things, and check the thermostat rating. The car should run near to the maximum of its recommended range — check the handbook for that data. The Capri runs between 185 and 216 degrees Fahrenheit, so we're running the 100E's V6 at 210 degrees.

The belt-driven stock fan on the average car engine is usually quoted as soaking up 4% of the engine's output. Bearing in mind longish waits in the fire-up lanes, it isn't too good an idea to try and do without a fan altogether, though maybe it's worth a trial run. A viscous free-feathering fan is better,

The electric fan on the 100E is mounted ahead of the rad so as to blow air through rather than suck air from behind. This set-up was necessary for reasons of radiator-to-mill clearance.

but still belt-driven (as fitted to many modern cars). The best answer is a thermostatically-operated electric fan which can be pre-set to your optimum temperature, and which will cut in and out to maintain it. Complete with all fittings and a manual override, a good electrical fan will weigh very little and cost about £50. Check mounting instructions; it can sit behind the rad and suck, as it were, or in front and blow.

Carburation/Manifolds

Attention to the inlet manifold is as important as attention to the carbs themselves — and in some cases merely relocating the stock carb on a new manifold may be enormously advantageous.

The manifold distributes the atomized petrol/air mixture from the carb to the combustion chambers. The efficiency with which it does this, and the equality with which it feeds all the cylinders, can vary for several reasons;

and on a stock motor is almost certainly such that considerable improvements (gained performance at the expense of economy, and replacing a simple casting which cost the manufacturer £3 with a specialist item costing ten times as much) can be made.

Manifold design — achieving optimum volumetric air/petrol vapour flow at all throttle settings — is a complex art, requiring flow-testing and provision for 'reversion', 'stand-off' and 'stagger-jetting'. The construction and finishing of an inlet manifold is no kitchen table job. Most V8s and larger engines such as V6s are catered for by the speed shops, as would be engines used by rally enthusiasts or any other obscure motor racing minority. If your engine is included in neither of those, consult one of the small number of carb specialists for a special application with regard to whatever carb set-up you have in mind.

There are several basic designs of inlet manifold. The most simple is the single-plane type. The gases are fed from the carb into a single commom chamber, which then distributes them to each cylinder. The drawback is that a cylinder is liable to be left short of petrol/air vapour by the cylinder which has just fired — especially if it is physically close to it.

A two-plane manifold is arranged so that separate channels cross over, feeding the vapour alternately on either side of the 'plenum divider'. The application — or even removal — of the divider dictates the engine's rpm-to-torque proportions to some degree. Throttle response will be quicker with a two-plane manifold as there is a smaller and smoother passage with less air to move out of the vapour's way. In the main, a two-planer improves mid-range torque, too.

An independent-runner, or isolated-runner manifold works like a two-plane unit, with a single smooth chamber for each cylinder, but rather than crossing over, the IR feeds downwards and is a 'high-rise' manifold. An IR manifold is for larger carbs, and allows the vacuum 'tunnel ram' effect to be used for tuning, which means that the higher the required torque peak, the shorter the tuned length. Hence tall IRs on American cars with bags of power and low torque ranges. Flashback can become considerable in a tall IR manifold, and is usually contained by a high stack above the carb.

A plenum-ram manifold looks much like an IR in section, but has a common plenum chamber above the point where the IR would end. Not only does this help to share out a large vapour capacity, but it also helps to dissipate the dangers of flashbacks. With a plenum-ram fitted to a dual-quad four two-choke carb set-up, each of four cylinders will be independently fed from four chokes mixing into one or two plenum chambers. Neither the plenum-ram nor the isolated runner style of manifold is really flexible enough for street use.

The excellent book on Holley carbs and manifolds published by H.P. Books makes a useful definition to end the confusion between hi-rise and hi-riser (American spelling) manifolds. Hi-riser means spacing the carb up from the manifold to ease and smooth out the flow passage. A hi-rise is a complete manifold which, as I mentioned with regard to IRs, has the runners mounted almost vertically so that the whole unit sits much higher.

Having now checked the three components of (a) engine application, (b) manifold suitability and performance degree, and (c) carburettor fitting, you can now move on to choose the right carb for your set-up. If you are going to try refitting the stock carb to a new manifold you will almost certainly have to alter the jets (do it while you're overhauling the thing). Check with your carb specialist or speed shop for help.

Carburation/The carb(s)

Discussing carb requirements is no easy job. The ground rules are few but basic, sure, but each application varies with both the car in question and exactly what you want to be asking of your engine. As a first move I followed my own advice and spoke to a speed shop specialist — Dave Grady at Super Power USA, just outside Leeds, Yorks. Given that I want to race my basically street-legal machine, I asked, where should I start with the carburation?

'If you're going to be content with just a bit of weekend fun and are really only starting out in dragging, I'd advise that you simply blueprint the existing carb as this will already be well-suited to your stock mill. You can either have it rebuilt by the local agents or have a crack at doing the job yourself. Get all the info you can find. Go through your manual carefully if you're doing this yourself, and ask the carb shop for a full overhaul kit. Carbs wear, just like anything else, and this'll give you new gaskets and seals as well as new jets. What you can check for, too, are bigger jets. In this way you can uprate the carb's performance but still get reasonable street use.

'A good middle road if you're modifying for more serious strip action would involve going for the largest jets in the range for an engine which was working at much higher revs overall. It's perfectly possible to have a street carb and a strip carb so long as you keep the linkages simple; most bolt to the manifold with only four studs and after you've driven to the strip it shouldn't take five minutes to hook up your racing carb. The drag-prepared carb will be a more efficient unit — by jetting for higher revs you'll be able to use a greater air/petrol vapour flow volume, but if you ran that on the street, stopping and starting and going through traffic, your plugs would be fouled up within a few minutes. In the States it's possible, taking things a

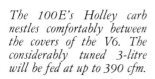

The 100E's Holley carb nestles comfortably between the covers of the V6. The considerably tuned 3-litre will be fed at up to 390 cfm.

stage further, for a racer to change his class simply by swapping his carbs over.

'I usually reckon as a rule of thumb that a full carb job can give an extra 10 bhp — and that's where you've got to start. A carb matched to a race manifold will give you another 20 bhp on the average middle-of-the-range street car. You can take that up to 30 bhp with headers, and go to a total increase of about 55 bhp if you add a good cam to the list.

'The air pattern coming to the carb is important. What you want is a smooth flow. A simple velocity stack will usually give you a level flow into the carb, but a good trick for starters is to remove the top half of the filter can, together with the filter, and leave the base plate of the can. This smooths the inlet flow to quite a degree and also shields the carb from hot air coming off the engine.' (More about this later.)

'A lot of people think that the answer to all their problems lies in simply bolting on a bigger carb. Lots more fuel doesn't mean lots more power — even if the carb is mated to the right manifold. Too many cars are choked, over-carburated. Get expert advice on matching the carb's performance to that of the motor in question.'

Dave has a couple of calculators to aid his judgment on supplying the right carb set-up to a customer, but I asked him — off the top of his head — what carburation he would recommend for a 3-litre V6 which had been moderately worked and where the owner wanted to move beyond the stock 2-barrel Weber. (Amercian carbs' performance is measured in cfm — cubic feet per minute — which is the carb's overall 'through-put' capacity.)

'The first thing to look at would be a single small Holley on a low manifold. I'd go for a larger 2-barrel rather than a much smaller 4-barrel in most cases. The recommended size would be between 350 and 390 cfm, but as they advise the 390 cfm for the 3½-litre Rover V8 as well, I'd tend to go for the 350 cfm. An interesting alternative would be a row of three Webers. Quite a good idea and easy to get hold of. I'd look to three twin-chokes so that you've got an effective 6-pack system, with the centre carb loaded and a progressive throttle action. This means that at the lower end of the rev range you'd be running on the centre carb, and beyond a certain point the linkages would bring in the other two. I've seen this set-up on several drag cars — very successfully on the original Liquidator Pop. I think the next thing to consider would be fuel injection. To get a unit from new would be very expensive, but it might be possible to get hold of a secondhand one from a current Granada.' (Although the Granada's bhp rating is less than that of a 3.0S Capri, the accleration figures are much the same despite the

Although fuel injection is very much the coming thing on high-performance production cars, it is still rare on drag machines. This Jaguar-powered rail uses the stock V12 injection set-up.

fact that the big saloon is carrying over 5 cwt more.)

A few words of explanation about the different types of carb. The 2-barrel Weber we mentioned, stock on the Capri, is a good place to start. It has two bores or holes running through it, which the Americans call barrels and which the British call chokes (not to be confused with what is often referred to as a 'choke' by people describing a cold-start carburettor assister). The 2-choke carbs are frequently referred to as twin-chokes, which isn't always accurate as they are not always of equal size (Webers and the like are identified by the diameter of their chokes — so a 28/28 is a twin-choke, and a 28/36 has a larger second barrel). A 4-barrel is simply a larger-bodied carb with the basic 2-barrel arrangement and a secondary barrel. The linkage opens the primary first. Then, when that one is about three-quarters open, the secondary barrel starts to open. You could draw the action on a graph. The primary would curve upwards and the secondary would start somewhere towards the top of the primary arc and then curve off more steeply. The primary would plateau fully open and the secondary would continue to arc up the graph until it, too, was right open and had peaked.

This all happens courtesy of the linkages, and for obvious reasons is called 'progressive'. As we saw when we mentioned the three twin-choke set-up, progressive throttle linkages also operate multi-carb systems, giving preference as required.

Some carbs, especially American ones, can come equipped with vacuum secondaries. These avoid the need for complex progressive linkages by opening the secondaries automatically. They work off the negative pressure in the manifold, which becomes greater as the engine revs increase (depression). Mechanical secondaries take up less space than do vacuum secondaries, and are correspondingly less complex, but for those linkages. A matter of personal preference, with no great advantages either way. A carb with vacuum-operated secondaries cannot be converted to mechanical operation.

One last expression often heard when folk are talking about American performance carbs is 'double pumper'. This refers to the carb's accelerator pump which governs the petrol flow into the unit. A double pumper has either two, or one with a greater capacity. These are only applicable to very high-revving race-only machines in almost every case; put another way, you are probably over-carbing your engine to use one on the street or in the lower classes.

Carburation/Air intake systems

An engine's volumetric efficiency is proportionately related to the density of the inlet air flow, such that the higher the density, the greater the rise in efficiency. Cold air is denser than warm air.

What that prize paragraph means in practice is that feeding cold air from outside the engine bay into the carb is better than merely letting it breathe the hot air coming off the block and manifolds. The temperature under the hood with the car at rest can be as high as 150 degrees Fahrenheit — and with every 11-degree decrease in that figure you'll gain about 1 horsepower (not *bhp*). There's always going to be quite a lot of heat — conducted through the metals, if nothing else — but the easy and cheap answer is an externally-aspirating cold-air feed.

Also, as we noted earlier, the smoother the air's passage into the carb, the better (just picture one of those wind-tunnel effects you've seen on *Tomorrow's World* where wild turbulence is smoothed out beautifully and to everyone's delight).

There are various systems. Dave Grady mentioned the old trick of removing all but the filter base plate; the stock air cleaner system will vary enormously, but it is worth taking a look at the set-up. Retaining a filter element of some sort — even if it's only a fine mesh — is a very good idea. It would only take a bit of gravel or similar debris to threaten your engine's very existence. Fine dust is rarely a problem for dragging purposes and would tend to go through the works unnoticed. Also, I know of more than one case of a nut or a stud being accidentally dropped into an open bellmouth and going unobserved — until it fused a piston to a bore, that is. Avoid the thin 'pancake' type of racing air filter, but those which are of a smaller diameter and are much taller (a couple of inches at least) are widely used. Some folks stay with their stock filter system and merely invert the top of the filter pan, so that more air can enter, but the aperture is still protected by the filter element.

Velocity stacks are just about the most common form of primary air intake system. In a complex IT manifold set-up they will form part of the tuned ram length, but they have a couple of advantages which are more widely applicable. Firstly, they are an efficient method of smoothing out the air flow into the carb; and secondly, by moving the intake up and away from the engine, it is possible to fit a hood scoop or air box of some sort — open-fronted — so that the carb is fed by fresh, cooler, air from outside the car. If the stack sits very high, allow at least a couple of inches between it and the top of the scoop or whatever for air circulation. Do not let the stack fit flush with the car's bodywork if you are merely cutting through the hood rather than building an air box around it. The natural aerodynamics will create a vacuum and starve off the air. Let the stack sit at least an inch higher.

A carefully designed hood scoop can provide a small amount of the 'ram air' effect so beloved of mid-Sixties American muscle cars. This is a sealed system which draws air through a hood scoop of some design and immediately funnels it down into the carb — either via a filter element or a stack. Not only does this provide external air, but the car's forward motion produces a slight 'ram' effect and forces the air into the carb with greater pressure as the car's speed increases.

Another low-buck trick which produces a slight ram force and feeds cold air to the carbs is to keep the stock filter box, remove the filter and, having cut one or two holes in the sides, glass-fibre or glue in one or two lengths of large-diameter tubing (such as flexible industrial vacuum cleaner piping), and then locate the far ends low down on the front of the car — under the bumper, say. A funnel of some sort on each entry is a good idea, and some type of filter will be essential. For a couple of pounds, though, you then get high-density cold air being forced through to the carbs under pressure. Filter box seals must be good and tight. For a filter I'd use a thin piece of foam between two pieces of mesh — and would keep a very close watch indeed on just how much dirt was getting picked up.

Carburation/Exotica

This book is not the right form to discuss the whys, wherefores, and how-muches of either supercharging or turbocharging. Their effect is to increase

Pick a header, any header, and then just pay for it? It's not that easy as application is all-important. Note how the tubes curve gradually and are all of equal length.

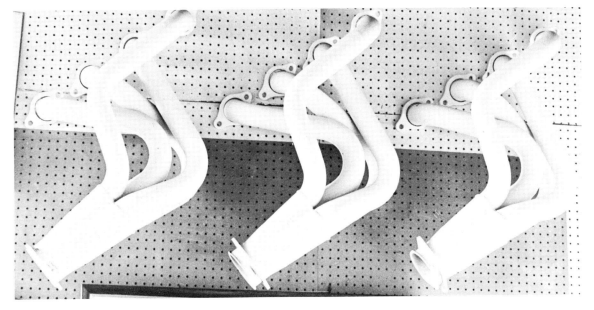

the pressure of the carburation system multi-fold, and their use gives dramatic results. Hardly tricks for our bracket/Street level, though. Don't be afraid of looking around at either set-up, however, with a view to the future; the Hocus Pocus Capri runs very successfully in the brackets at New York Dragway with its turbocharged 302, and there's an old-type Granada running at Long Marston with a simple supercharger on the stock mill.

Nitrous oxide injection cannot be overlooked, though. It's the 'magic' passport to bolt-on, flick-a-switch-and-go, instant power. It *can* give you 50% more power and take two seconds off your ETs.

The combustible oxygen is more easily extracted and ignited from nitrous oxide (laughing gas) than from boring old air, and with a proportionate increase in petrol supply can be set up on virtually any basically solid engine — injected straight into the inlet manifold — so that a flick of a switch feeds it into the system. A complete unit will cost at least £300-£400 and it is best to get advice from an expert supplier/fitter. Nitrous oxide is legal for bracket racing, but is still a grey area in class racing. Check it out; and where illegal don't try hiding it — s'naughty.

Headers

Headers are the exhaust manifolds which carry away the engine's waste gases. The more efficiently this process is conducted, the better the engine's performance. The exhaust leaves the combustion chambers under pressure and racing headers take greater advantage of this to get the gases flowing away rapidly. There are several ways in which they achieve this.

Firstly, they comprise a separate tube for each chamber or cylinder which eliminates the turbulence of gas flow as found in a conventional manifold. Headers are constructed in such a way that each pipe is of equal length so that all the cylinders have an equal back-pressure and the 'pulsing' of the engine doesn't favour particular cylinders. The curves in the pipes describe far less acute angles than in stock outlet manifolds so that the gases flow more smoothly and, again, turbulence is reduced dramatically. Finally, the collector — the box within which the tubes terminate — is designed in such a way that it helps draw the exhaust out quicker still.

Take a look at the standard manifold. It's probably made of cast-iron and pours the gases from all the cylinders, or one bank of a V-engine, into a single pipe, and then forces the exhaust through a succession of very tight corners and bends. It's not difficult to imagine the turbulence which sets up in there — all of which defeats the object of drawing the waste out quickly to leave a purer petrol vapour/air mix in the cylinder so that each sparked explosion is unimpaired by waste burned gas. Headers should be up on your list of engine modifications and, being bolt-on items, are easily installed.

Header size needs to be a compromise, especially in terms of internal tube diameter and overall tube length. The longer, smaller-diameter types will provide low-rev torque and flexibility, while shorter and wide headers will allow higher revs. The latter is obviously the better bet for dragging, but isn't going to be too practical for street use. The headers on the 100E are indicative of a good compromise. Each tube is 30 inches long, so that the 9 to 12-inch collectors are positioned just ahead of the rear of the gearbox, and have an internal diameter of 1½ inches (and 2¾ inches on the extractors).

Headers for V8s and popular racing engines can often be bought 'off the shelf' at a speed shop. If nothing is immediately available for your engine there are two alternatives. The first is to have a set custom made by a specialist — phone for a price, it may not be as prohibitively expensive as you might have thought. Or, secondly, self-weld header kits are just becoming available. With these you get a succession of components which need piecing together (with expert welding) to form the optimum header.

There are a couple of things to look out for. Avoid very cheap headers which are made of thin-walled steel. Not only will these have a much shorter life, but will also give a less deep resonant engine note than a good quality header. Wall thickness should be around 1/16-in. For most applications, though, the biggest problem with headers on a Street or Production car is clearance. Check this very carefully, look for spark plug clearance, steering clearance, and proximity to any ancillaries which could be damaged or adversely affected by the heat. Dennis acquired a weld-up kit from GDS Exhausts for the 100E and took them up and over rather than down and under because of problems with the cross-member and the steering system, and then he had to change all the plug leads to L-shaped terminals to avoid the danger of the leads burning.

Having carefully selected your headers and being certain of their ability to slip easily (or less easily, but at least successfully) on to the motor, you will probably find that they are supplied in bare metal. Paint it. Chroming isn't really recommended; chrome holds heat and unless it is of very high quality will blue and burn off very quickly. Nickel plating is a possibility — ask your local plater, but be prepared to wince at the price.

Obviously the headers must be completely cleaned and degreased prior to painting. Shot or bead blasting is a good idea, but a chemical solvent will do. Hang them up in a garage and give them two or three coats of Very High Temperature paint, following the instructions on the can fastidiously. Get a good VHT, too; to have to take them off and do the job again in a fortnight's time would be a big yawn. When the pipes first get hot some surface paint will burn off; don't worry, it'll soon settle down.

It is now worth checking the pipe openings where they are welded to the flange which bolts to the engine block. Any welding drips or irregular contours around the openings should be carefully filed off. Do not go mad

On the 100E, the GDS headers curve up to the rocker cover height and then drop away sharply behind the mill.....

.....to end in collectors which pass level with the back of the auto transmission. A tricky application.

with a grinder on a drill; you may weaken the join or even go through the pipe wall.

When installing the headers ensure that you use a new gasket and suffcient silencer-joining gum at the block end to ensure a really gas-proof fit. Leaking gases will ruin the whole effect. With the headers in place check again for proximity to ancillaries and fuel lines or even brake pipes. Satisfied? Good. We can now consider the rest of the exhaust system.

You don't need one. Not for dragging. That's the short answer. But of course you do need silencers and exit pipes for street use, and the choice is to either fabricate a quick unhook system, fit cut-outs, or fit the silencing system which least affects your engine's performance and race with it in place.

The problem with a quick-unhook system is to get a good seal between the collector flange and the silencer pipe flange. It can be done, and a spring-loaded clip on either side of each connection helps. If you've not skipped the chapter in which we raced the Mustang you'll recall the difficulty we had removing the exhaust on that. Obviously an in-pit unhook exhaust system must come away with the least possible fuss. Sorting rear fastenings so that the mounting rubbers slide away or are held in place by quick-release pins or even wing nuts is no problem and only needs a little ingenuity.

Cut-outs are valves which fit between the collectors and the silencer pipes. Operated by cables from inside the car, they allow the gases to either flow through the silencing system or to be diverted so that they exit immediately. Cut-outs are rather out of fashion, and such a set-up doesn't have the weight-shedding advantage of an unhook system.

Silencers need not be enormously restrictive. Performance units will almost invariably be a trifle loud for road use, though, and racing with them *in situ* you're still carrying the weight. The gas flow in a normal silencer follows a W-pattern and the exhaust doesn't get away as quickly as it might. In a performance silencer the gases either go straight through — the pipe lined with herring-bone baffles or the like — or follow a low-restriction S-shape. The choice is yours, but I would take the application to an expert for an opinion on the individual case — pipe lengths and diameters and silencer positioning are all pretty critical and need to be just so for maximum efficiency. Avoid flexible exhaust tubing; the ribbing causes internal turbulence.

Some time ago I mentioned the tinny tone of cheap headers. A strange point, granted, but it's a nice plus to get your racer sounding right. The open-headers route on a V8 growls and grumbles on low revs — and makes an unforgettable roar off the line. Good for your ego and for the crowd. Burble, burble, burble, burble . . .

Ignition

The engine in your car — and my car come to that — is of a desperately crude design. The prototypes were built more than 100 years ago and there have been few fundamental advances within the last 50 years. The internal combustion engine has many inherent weaknesses, not least among which is the critical nature of the ignition fire. To explode the petrol vapour/air mixture, each spark plug has to deliver a spark of the correct size, in the right place within the cylinder, and at exactly the right moment relative to the engine's cycle of internal movement . . . and get it right, for each spark plug, more than 1,000 times every minute (maximum revs on a V6)

It is definitely worth paying attention to your ignition system; not only will you benefit greatly from getting as close as you can to optimum ignition firing, which makes best use of the engine's capability, but even the slightest degree of error or weakness in the system will lose you power or cause misfiring — at the very least.

Within the coil a magnetic field is set up by current from the car's electrical generating system passing through two sets of unequally-packed windings. This boosts the voltage to create sufficient momentum for the ignition process to commence. A stock coil will hardly be up to the job for serious racing, as well as being potentially weak. A heavy-duty racing coil

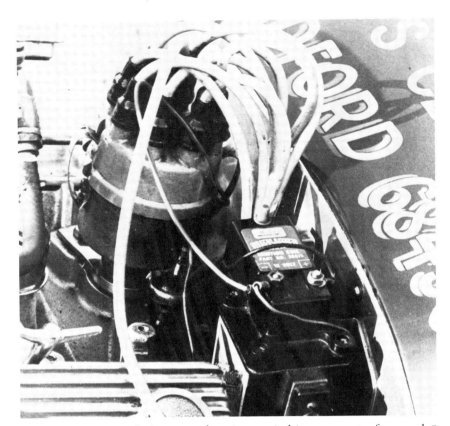

will generate around 40,000 volts via a switching current of around 8 amperes; sufficient to install and forget on virtually any engine. These comp coils will probably feature oil-filled cases and be made of shock-resistant materials — and have really positive (no pun intended) connections.

This high voltage from the coil is despatched to the centre of the distributor, where it is literally distributed via the rotor arm, between the HT (high tension) leads, which then take it to the respective plugs. There are two weaknesses here. Firstly, the physical action of the distributor is unimpressive, relying as it does on the bent wire of the rotor to make contact with the various HT connections. Secondly, the contact breaker points which make up the circuit. The voltage is not required as a constant flow, and the points operate as a valve — regulated by the timing of the engine itself. The actuation of the points is purely mechanical; spring-loaded, they physically open and close — and any variation in the gap between the 'face' and the 'heel' (the areas which make the contact) will reduce the efficiency. When the points are closed, current flows into the primary (input) side of the coil — this is point dwell. When they open, the circuit breaks and this is the points gap. The timing of the ignition will vary if they open or close too quickly, and anyway they get dirty and are subject to bounce and incorrect alignment by the very nature of their mechanical structure.

Answer? Throw the lot away. This is where we meet contactless electronic ignition. The magazines are full of adverts for 'magic' 'lecky ignition systems, but the only kind which is of any interest at all is that which completely replaces the points. The action of the rotor arm and its inadequacies can be replaced with a magnetic pickup system or with an 'optical' LED and photo-transistor set-up. The choice between optical and magnetic systems is up to you; both operate with capacitor discharge systems (CD) which increase both the voltage and the coil's efficiency. Applications are available for just about every engine, and they either bypass the contact breakers or replace them entirely. Kits of complete cam-operated distributor units and matched coils (sometimes called transformers in the American catalogues) can be bought over the counter for every American V8 likely to be found dragging.

Condensers are worth a brief mention. The condenser is a sort of shock absorber which irons out any sudden bursts of current in the system. Replace if necessary, though the equipment mentioned above will include provision for a condenser of some form.

Having successfully generated all this ignition power, it's now important that it gets to the plugs without hiccup or hindrance. The HT leads and their terminals all want checking. Old HT leads tend to get brittle. Old terminals tend to loosen. Very heavy-duty silicone HT lead is available, as are spark caps and distributor terminals (with heat resisting qualities, and the ability to shrug off petrol, oil and water). Do check the metal connectors within each plug cap or the way in which the cap threads into the braid within the lead.

Lead separators which keep the HT leads tidy and help to avoid them being confused and crossed when the plugs are out are a good idea. So, to, are lead markers; little tabs on each lead which indicate the firing order. And while you are spending your pocket money at the speed shop, ignition timing tape is available, which, being self-adhesive, goes round the crank pulley to indicate top dead centre (TDC) and the degrees to either side.

Plugs, finally. The last link in the ignition chain. One per cylinder is a grand idea . . . but which ones?

For a start, no plug in itself will give you better performance, but as you increase the engine's capabilities in other departments you need to make sure that the spark plugs' capacity is sufficient to keep pace. Plug condition is critical. Plug gaps must be exact and the earth electrode must sit squarely over the centre electrode so that the spark occurs in precisely the right place. Neither electrode must be burned down by excessive hot use. Plug condition is easily gauged by sight. A black and oily wet plug with a residue which will not rub off indicates oil fouling — oil in the chamber being burnt off, check for a worn valve guide, rings not seated or broken, detonation, or a broken valve or spring. If the plug's nose (the ceramic around the centre) is dark grey or black, and there is a dry fluffy deposit round the edge, the problem is fuel fouling; the mixture may be too rich, that plug may be bad, as may its HT lead, or — if all the plugs are in this condition — the ignition is too weak or the plugs are of the wrong heat range. Overheating will be shown by a bleached-white plug with 'boiling' round the centre electrode, and there may also be dark spots or a satin sheen on the nose. This points to too lean a mixture, incipient pre-ignition, inadequate engine cooling, excessive spark advance, or, again, the wrong plug for the job or detonation. The larger the 'boil', and where the metal edges are speckled

American performance equipment is readily available over the speed shop counter for many applications in addition to the familiar V8 installations.

and specks are appearing on the nose or elecrodes, the greater the evidence of detonation.

The perfect used spark plug has clean electrodes, no 'cement boil' on the nose, a clean metal surround, and a white-ish tan or brown colour to the insulator nose. For racing purposes do not bother putting in hours of work finely cleaning a set of bad plugs; throw them away and start with correctly-gapped new ones. Never use plugs which have been damaged in any way or even dropped. Don't remove them from their packaging until you need them, and wire-brush and then cloth-wipe them after a day's racing. The spark plug is simple in its construction but more delicate than most people think — and certainly of great importance as far as its condition goes.

So which plug? The easy answer is that each application is a one-off and you should 'phone up someone like Champion and speak to their technical department, describing the engine modifications and purposes, and ask their advice. If you have taken your engine to a high state of tune then that really is what I would suggest you do. Broad guidelines are possible, though.

Spark plugs are available with insulator noses of various lengths. The shorter the nose, the 'colder' the plug as it dissipates its heat rapidly. A 'hot' plug has a long nose and retains more heat. If your car's engine is highly tuned and therefore generates more heat in the cylinders — and racing camshafts, a higher compression ratio and/or modified ignition (plus, of course, supercharging) are the most important factors quoted by Champion with regard to combustion chamber temperature — you will generally be looking to a 'colder' plug so that the heat can be transferred into the block as quickly as possible. The higher the plug's number, the hotter its application. The standard 3-litre Capri runs N9Ys, which is relatively hot for road use; you would be looking — as a generalization — to move towards 7s or 6s. Though, as their technical adviser pointed out, given certain engine conditions he might just as easily be advising a hotter plug; but that's the principle. On a stock motor do not change far if at all from the recommended plug.

Some teams (*all* fuel teams) use 'warm-up' plugs to bring the engine up to its optimum temperature more quickly. These plugs can be allowed to foul while carb tuning or whatever is going on, and then be swopped just before racing begins. In the main, stick to the recommended gap on the plug, though Champion suggest reducing road plug gaps by 0.005 in in some cases. Don't go beyond that.

Instruments

Having got the mill all hopped-up and smart, you now need a couple of good quality gauges to tell you what it's doing and warn you of impending disaster, and all you basically require is a tachometer (rev counter) and an oil-pressure gauge.

The positioning of these two instruments is as important as any other factor. If you look at a standard-mounted gauge and then up at the road, you'll find you've probably had to shift your vision through as much as 35 degrees, as well as refocus from a distance of 18 inches to infinity. The movement of the head and the blink of the eyes has taken time — not a lot, sure, but enough for you to have missed your green light. And, on a very bright day, you'll find yourself blinking at the low-mounted deep-set dials for a moment before the pupils open far enough to cope with the relative darkness.

You can do a lot about the angle and the light contrast by locating the tachometer (and possibly the oil-pressure gauge, too) either on top of the dashboard or in the back of the hood scoop if you have one. See now? It's just a flick of the eye . . . indeed it's possible to set things up so that when you are staring straight ahead you can still catch both the tacho's needle and the lights of the christmas tree on the periphery of your field of vision.

One smart dodge I've seen several times is to leave the oil-pressure gauge in its usual position, but relocate the oil warning light. Mount an old single-unit stop light or whatever — big as you like — on top of the dash, and wire it up instead of (or as well as) the stock oil warning light. If you get a problem the thing'll glow like a beacon.

The tachometer is the most important instrument on your race car. You drive *by* it, and, crucially, shift by it. A speedometer is of no interest to you at all. On one occasion I drove a Street car which was fitted with matching tacho and speedo, and more than once my eyes were distracted by seeing *two* leaping needles — I blanked the speedo off with masking tape in the end.

Tachometers fall into two types. The first is cable-driven, like a speedo, and the second works on electronic impulse — its three wires connect to earth, live feed and the ignition coil lead. The electronic type is generally more efficient and faster in operation.

As for digital tachos — if you are used to them and like their action, fine. It's like getting used to a digital watch, I suppose. I don't like digital tachos; there's room for error in misreading the figures. With a sweep needle on a dial you don't tend to look so much as which figure the needle is against, but at the needle's position in itself. You can't do that with digitals — though there are American units with pre-set capabilities which flash an LED display at you when it's time to shift gear.

A good electronic tacho will cost you about £25, though you can pay £35 to £45 as you enter the really sophisticated areas of high(ish) technology, and the tacho being such a vital instrument I would tend to spend the money.

Competition tachos are available with multiple functions. The first thing to do is to set the red line at your rev limit (6,000 on the 100E for example), the top of the power curve, or if you prefer, the point at which the car's engine stops producing power and starts to destroy itself. Racers not only have an experienced ear to detect the rev peaks through the gears, but also pay meticulous attention to their tachos. A comp tacho may well have a separate 'shift light' which relates to the red-line setting and illuminates when it has decided that it is right for you to grab the next gear. Another refinement is a 'maximum revs indicator'. This is like the max half of a max/min thermometer; the main needle pushes a second needle, so that after you have stopped, this second needle will still be indicating your highest rev reading. Comes in two types, to be re-set either by a push-button release or by the use of a key.

The ultimate competition tacho must be those such as are made by Mallory, which feature an engine safety control. Such controls are available as independent units; they take the pulse from the ignition coil lead and if the engine touches a dangerously high rev limit, it switches the engine off until the revs drop. Accidental mis-shifting, for example, can result in a spinning tacho needle — and expensive damage. The ace tachometer not only includes the safety control facility, but goes a technical step beyond. Instead of switching off the engine it limits its increased performance over a certain figure, but gradually, by removing spark firing and increasing that removal as the revs get more dangerous. Mallory call it 'Proportional Control', and I call it damn clever.

When you've got all that sorted — and paid for — you've got all the instrumentation you need. Being a cautious sort of chap, though, there are two more instruments I would include — a fuel gauge and a water-temperature gauge — just so that I'd know. They can be positioned any old place, though. All of which makes quite a nice change from the days of Mini-Coopers and Lotus Cortinas when you *had* to have three dozen supplementary gauges — compasses, altimeters, traffic warden detectors, geiger counters and directional crumpet-finding dials . . . and those black plastic extended levers that fitted over the switches. Remember them? Gosh, you must be as old as I am.

Pre-race routine tune-up

There is an old adage which suggests that if something's going right, don't mess with it or you'll only foul it up. There's a lot of truth in that, but regardless, I would recommend going through a tuning check list before each race meeting. Preferably on the morning of the meet, at the strip itself

— air temperature and humidity can affect things like carb settings.

(1) Check tyre pressures front and rear (while still cold). Optimum slick pressures will vary, but work out your favourite psi taking the manufacturer's recommendation as a base.

(2) Check the engine oil level and its condition.

(3) Check that you've got enough petrol in the tank for the meeting.

(4) Check the engine cooling system where applicable — especially if you are bracket racing and may have to run frequently.

(5) Check the spark plugs — yes, even the difficult to reach ones up by the firewall.

(6) Check the engine timing, the ignition system and that all leads are making good connections.

(7) Where applicable check valve clearances.

(8) Check the carb(s). Adjust if necessary, but do look at throttle linkages and how well the carb is breathing. If a choke is fitted ensure that it is completely off when running at race temperature, whether manually operated or automatic.

(9) Check the battery's condition and its connections.

(10) Glance under the car. Gravity is a wonderful thing, and oil or trans fluid falls downward, as do loose cables or . . . whatever.

Finally, with the engine warm, just cruise the car carefully around the pits and give it a short blast in the 'play-pen'. How does it feel? No lumps in the transmission or drivetrain? Is the engine sounding right and breathing happily right through the rev range?

Yes? Good. You're in business and bound for glory.

Spending the money

Budgeting to build a drag car is no easy matter — nor, for that matter, is any hard-and-fast cash limit ever particularly applicable. American magazines seem to come up with a 'Go Dragging For Fifteen Bucks' feature every six months or so. Indeed, given a fire extinguisher, a crash helmet, a good safety harness (probably the standard fixture), and the costs of an RAC licence, club membership and race entry, you can ignore this entire carefully researched and impressively lengthy chapter and just run up and race. Folk do.

Apart from those who race hire cars or their company cars, though, no-one can resist the temptation to make their machine more competitive. And it isn't really valid for me to tell you how to apply £500 to your

It really need not cost an arm and a leg. I'm not being anything but complimentary about the owner of this small Ford Modified when I say that it's a good example of a budget racer.

car to turn it into an interesting racer. Guys don't merely remove the cash from their piggy bank in a lump sum; building at this level is an evolutionary process, governed by factors such as whether you can persuade your mum that you *did* pay her for your keep the other day.

There again, costs fluctuate. At some point you will come across something really boring and insignificant, but vital, which requires far more cash than it could ever merit in race terms. On the other hand, once you start getting into the sport and asking around, folk do you deals and bits turn up at the right time and at the right price.

To demonstrate priorities, though, rather than cash investment, let's assume that you've given me an old Mustang with a healthy 289, and told me to spend £150 and take it racing on as competitive a basis as possible. Rather than tuning and fiddling, I'd be looking for a reliable and consistent car which was capable of putting down all its available power cleanly and efficiently. With more of an eye on bracket racing rather than class racing, this is how I would spend the money:

Lightening. Need cost nothing at all.	£0
Pre-loading rear suspension by adding or subtracting a leaf, adding Teflon strips, or adjusting shackle lengths.	£5
Simple traction bars. Probably bolt-up style.	£20
Change oil filter. Top up diff level.	£10
Basic tune-up. Electrics, plugs, points, etc.	£25
Simple carb rebuild. New jets and gaskets.	£25
Carb breathing. Stack or direct cold-air system.	£10
Build quick-release catches on to exhaust system.	£5
Fire extinguisher.	£20
Crash helmet.	£30

Which would add up to £150, and I'd be in business. Had you then allowed me to spend more time and money on the car progressively over the season, my personal list of priorities would run as follows:

Carburation up-rate and new manifold.	£70
Headers.	£40
Ladder bars and rear air shocks.	£120
90/10 front shocks.	£80
Glass-fibre bonnet and boot and further lightening.	£50
Slicks.	£200
Shifter.	£30
Electronic ignition.	£20
Racing tacho and oil-pressure gauge.	£40
Uprated transmission.	
Engine internals and a smart cam.	

All but the last two items would bring the bill to a total of £650. Not getting too ambitious with the mill and trans work might just allow you to own a really neat and very respectable quick 289 Muzzie for £1,000 — and that's assuming new parts in every case. £1,000 is £20 a week over a year — which is a good deal of money, but not beyond many people's capabilities. Also, look what you'll have to show for it as the car builds up over the months; never missing a meeting, but getting faster and more consistent as the season goes on.

Bolt-on Survival

SAFETY SYSTEMS

Drag racing, overall, is one of the safest of motor sports. There are only ever two cars racing at one time, both are heading in the same direction at much the same sort of speed and there are no corners — so crashes are relatively rare, and when they do occur it is generally as a result of vehicle failure of some sort. And when an accident happens on a drag strip it can never be far from — let alone out of sight of — the fire tender, the ambulances and the marshals. I have seen the rescue crews going into action on several occasions and have always been impressed by their speed and efficiency.

After any sort of crash, speed is all-important. I could not envisage the rescue crews taking more than 30 seconds to get to an incident anywhere on the strip — which may sound like a long time if you're stuck in a burning car, but a similar facility at the Isle of Man TT or even at the highly-organized circuit racing meetings could save many lives at those venues.

It's worth knowing how the rescue crews work when they arrive at an incident. Their first concern, above all others, is the safety of the driver. To this end they'll tear your car apart if they have to. The first thing they look for are the ignition cut-off (even if the engine has stopped) and the battery isolation switch so that they can kill the flow of current which could start a fire. If they can't see an isolation switch they will take the bonnet and/or boot lid off — using bolt cutters if necessary, and slice through the battery leads. At the same time the marshals will be getting you out of the car by whatever means are necessary and handing you to the ambulancemen. At the slightest suspicion of fire they will move in with their high-capacity extinguishers.

There are obvious basic steps which you can take to help them . . . just in case. From this point of view, quick-release hood pins are a good idea, as is an external battery isolator, which will only set you back £10-£12. The battery itself must be securely located with metal straps. The earth lead from the battery must be coloured yellow (wrap it round with insulating tape), and all these safety aids must be signposted. You can buy sheets of handy self-adhesive decals which include flash-symbols for the battery or the isolator, on/off arrows for the ignition switch, and big red Es to denote earth leads. Being universal and thus needing no explanation, these decals are probably a better idea than simply signwriting in the information.

As far as specific safety systems go, the rules dictate what is required for your level of racing — and that's the minimum. Never cut corners or allow yourself to be tempted towards false economy where safety is concerned. The temptation to buy a cheap seat belt so that you're left with more money to spend on the engine is understandable, but really dumb.

Crash helmets are obligatory in every class and in bracket racing (even for truck drivers). For all car racing the helmet must comply with the British Standards Institute's BS 2495-77. And if you think you can get past the scrutineer with one of inferior grade, I can tell you from experience you'll be wrong.

Helmets come in various guises. The most common is the bike-type of

'full face' helmet which comes right round over the chin. Dennis has one of that style, but I prefer my 'open face' type; much less claustrophobic and less likely to make you sweat cobs when you're waiting in the fire-up lane on a hot summer afternoon.

The shell of the helmet will be made from either glass-fibre or polycarbonate — the choice is yours, though the material will dictate the price. One thing to note, though, is that the structure of polycarbonate helmets is weakened by paint or even stickers, and many people are deeply suspicious of the material anyway.

Crash helmets start in price at about £30, you should be able to get a really good one for £50, and at the far end of the scale, £170 will buy you a real 'state of the art' American helmet with fully-fireproof Nomex lining and flame vents in the front breather piece. Drivers of cars without full windscreens must wear splinter-proof goggles or visors.

Seats belts, safety harness — call them what you will. Don't mess around with lap or lap-diagonal belts, but get a full-race four-point harness. These are so called because they bolt to the car in four places. The harness itself comprises two straps which come straight down over the shoulders and attach to the waist bands, and join in the middle with a quick-release buckle. On really good harnesses this waist section and the buckle will have a detachable pad to cushion the shock to the stomach area. A full set-up of this type will cost between £25 and £30. Very good value for money.

Myself, I would tend to keep away from inertia-reel seat belts for racing (though static belts infuriate me in normal driving), if only because the inertia mechanism is a component which can fail, and a static belt completely eliminates that admittedly unlikely possibility.

Take great care installing the harness. Sit right back in your seat and check that you can reach all the instruments and switches without straining forward. If the floor mounts of the conventional seat belt on either side of you are in the right place, use them. Take the back straps to the floor, the roll cage, the back shelf, or somewhere equally solid and mount them as securely as possible on the thickest metal. Check that the straps won't catch or snag, and if you're bolting the mounts through the floor or rear shelf reinforce the back of the sheet metal with body washers or a small plate of at least $\frac{1}{4}$-inch thickness. Install the belts while at mid-adjustment and check the adjustment twice over before drilling and bolting. There's a Securon four-point belt in the 100E — it's of impressive quality, and comes complete with its own threaded back plates which spread the load over a large area when under strain. Fixing bolts must be steel, and have a minimum diameter of $\frac{5}{16}$-in.

A fire extinguisher is an essential. There are various types available, the main difference being in the chemical content. Dry powder, propelled by carbon dioxide, is the cheapest, but is not recommended by the RAC. They prefer BCF, Freon, or pure carbon dioxide — and, by the way, specify a

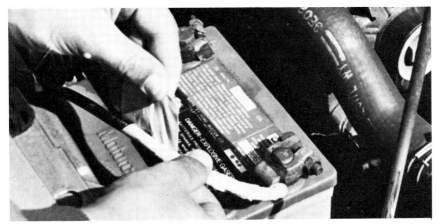

To satisfy the scrutineer when racing the Capri we had to wrap the earth lead with yellow tape. This makes one of the first tasks of a rescue crew's routine much easier.

The four-point safety harness in the 100E, adjusted to allow a little movement, but so that there is no chance of the driver making contact with dash or windscreen on impact. The two top straps pass through the seat, then across once to avoid snagging, and bolt to the rear shelf.

Right to hand on a simple spring clip any time we need it. The trigger-style operation of the 100E's BCF extinguisher is efficient and unambiguous in its direction-ability.

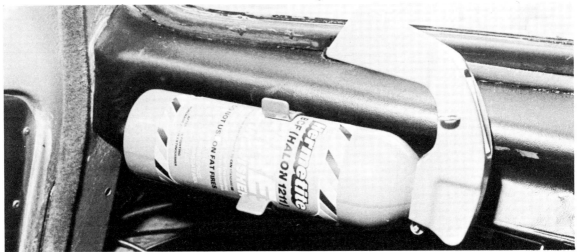

minimum weight of 1 kilogram. The extinguisher must be securely mounted in an easily-reached position, but must be held by a quick-release catch. A 2-kg BCF extinguisher will cost you more than £20, and a large metred 5-kg BCF unit around £75. BCF, though, is very 'clean' in operation and doesn't leave all the mess associated with dry-powder extinguishers.

Another form of fire extiguisher is the professional plumbed-in system, where lines take the BCF or whatever to the engine, the fuel tank, the battery and wherever else you might need it. The operation can either be triggered automatically or manually, so that should fire break out you can jump clear yourself and leave the sprinkler system spraying away behind you. It costs well over £100, but is very good insurance.

A variation on the theme is one of the available life support systems. This is a small self-contained unit which automatically pumps pure air into the driver's crash helmet as soon as a fire has started. Another £100s worth, and though hardly applicable to Street cars, I'd not see the lid of a Funny Car come down over my head without something of the sort. If you want to use one, mount the unit on the door side of you rather than in the middle of the car, so that your umbilical cord will stay with you for a couple of feet as you eject rather than having to part company as soon as you leave your seat.

Finally, as far as extinguishers are concerned, we have a regulation BCF extinguisher in the car, but also keep a small domestic aerosol extinguisher in the tool box for the incidents that can occur when working on the engine . . . or whatever; definitely better safe than sorry. Fire is not fun.

While I am on the subject of fire, it's worth mentioning petrol cans. Yes, really. Fire is a considerable danger, and the place where fire is most likely to start is in your petrol — be that petrol in the car's tank or in your reserve supply.

Explosion-proof mesh-filled petrol cans might seem like an extravagance, and indeed old oil cans serve just as well in the usual run of events. When those events include someone dropping their cigarette, or when a spark is thrown up from whatever source, you'll be glad that you bothered to get something like our Paddy Hopkirk Explosafe can. Or not, as the smouldering case may be.

Checking through the race car's fuel system and refitting the plumbing with high-performance components is well worth the time, effort and money; both to ensure against leaks on the grounds of safety, and to ensure that the vital fluid has a clear passage to the engine. The rule book dictates that all cars shall have a metal firewall between the tank and the driver's compartment as well.

Roll bars, roll cages; only obligatory for open cars in the lower classes and bracket racing, but a very good idea right across the board. Drag cars in classes below Competition Altered don't tend to go out of control and roll with any frequency, but it has happened, and without a roll cage you'll find the roof collapsing and piercing headaches ensuing.

There's not much in the way of magic ingredients when it comes to a roll cage. A local engineering shop with a heavy-duty tube-bender could make one up for you — the tube to be of adequate diameter and wall, and to terminate in four-bolt plates to mount to a secure area of the car's floor or wherever.

The simplest of cages will comprise a hoop which follows the roof contours and bolts to the floor just behind the seats (watch for crash helmet clearance). The next step would be one or two bracing bars running down a diagonal to the rear of the car. Then either one central forward bracing strut, or one low-level strut coming across the bottom of the doors. Possibly a cross-brace behind the seats, too.

There are a couple of specialist roll cage manufacturers, and prices range from £30 to about £100. Cages can be supplied in either steel or a lighter alloy, and comply with RAC regulations as a matter of course. Cages for popular types of car are available off the peg, as it were, and can be ordered direct from the makers or through a good local speed shop.

Owen Hayward all dressed up and ready to go in fire suit, fireproof gloves and boots, helmet, goggles and breathing mask. Note the harness and handle for the fire extinguisher system in the top left corner.

A very good idea is to pad the roll cage — especially across the top where it is most likely to come into contact with your head. Preformed padded rubber strips are available — a slit tube which you simply slip on to the bar and then secure with tie-grips.

The rule book dictates that the roll cage must be no more than 6 inches behind and 3 inches above the driver's helmeted head. Braces must be of the same diameter and wall thickness as the main member. Where roll cages are mandatory, excepting cars manufactured before 1972, the dimensions must be as follows: Up to 2 litres — 1 inch or 1¼-inch diameter by .09-inch wall; up to 4 litres — 1½-inch diameter by .09-inch wall; and over 4 litres — 1⅝-inch diameter by .09-inch wall. Cars made before 1972 must comply to 1¾-inch diameter by .065-inch wall thickness. Roll cages for Dragsters, Funny Cars and Comp Altereds must be made of seamless steel tubing.

Clothing. Must be worn, for a start. Driving in the nude to reduce rolling weight is not specifically banned by the rule book, but the girls in the crowd would only snigger. What the bible does say is that arms, legs and torso up to the neck must be covered with 'suitable clothing'. Single-layer fire-resistant overalls and gloves are obligatory in all classes other than Street and Production — though it is 'strongly recommended' there, too.

Drivers of front-engined cars running nitro-methane must wear an approved fire suit and a full face mask which incorporates a filter. Drivers of other Dragsters and Competition Altereds must wear a mask which would prevent the inhalation of flames.

Fire suits start on the far side of £50, lined with Nomex or Proban material. Then there's the Nomex underwear, too. Fireproof boots cost between £60 and £110, while the gloves to make up the set will cost you at least another £20 — a pricey business, sure, but it's certainly what the well-turned-out Funny Car jockey is wearing this year.

The single most inflammable item inside your car is almost certainly your seat, and you're going to be sat right on top of it (well, in it). If you're dedicated to emptying your off-shore account you can spend £135 on a Corbeau GT8 racing seat — covered with Nomex and completely flameproof. Guaranteed not to warm the cockles of your heart, as it were.

To conclude this chapter on safety I'll just dip back into the NDRC's rule book. It's all self-obvious really and when you come to race you can get your own copy to learn about ballast and the regulations concerning glass-fibre floors (must be steel reinforced), but it is worth quoting the two paragraphs which lead into their section on safety:

'All cars must be scrutineered to establish that they have been prepared to a suitably safe standard to be raced. Failure to comply with any of the safety regulations will be grounds for rejection at scrutineering and any change made after passing scrutineering is grounds for immediate disqualification. The scrutineer's decision on any matter is final.

'All cars must be presentable at all times. Cars that are considered to be improperly prepared may be rejected at scrutineering. In particular, the steering and braking systems must be presented at scrutineering in a clean condition, with any flexible hydraulic hose free from paint.'

It all stands to reason — and the reason is your safety.

Don't Pick the Cherries

WHAT TO TAKE TO THE STRIP

Just about the worse thing in the world — far worse than being laughed at by the scrutineer, and on par with being laughed at by your girlfriend — is having five minutes to go before the final and finding you're short of a cross-head screwdriver or one N9Y. The following list is not total and does include a couple of luxury items, but it is the sort of kit you should be looking to. It amounts to a large amount of money as capital outlay, but costs can be cut and the majority of the equipment may be built up over a period of time. Start hinting like mad just before Christmas. This is what *we* take with us when we go dragging — together, needless to say, with our famed entourage of blonde-haired, long-legged, hefty-chested groupies.

Petrol
Obvious. Four gallons should be enough to see you through a day's racing. These explosion-proof and totally fume-sealed pro cans are a very good idea as I said in the chapter on safety.

Water
Jolly useful stuff. For both cars and people. I used to brew beer in a seven-gallon plastic barrel until I realized it was tainting the brew. It's a good capacity and is usefully fitted with a tap — and it now sees drag service.

Oil
We always have two gallons of Duckhams with us. At least. And that should be enough for all but Pro Stock upwards.

Socket set
Indispensable. Ours came from Kenward Tools. Not an item to try and economize over.

Jump leads
Get ones with heavy positive clips and the longest possible cables.

Spare battery
Useful, especially if you are running the car without a charging system. Store it well away from petrol and the like.

Winch
A Haltrac Sherpa winch. Very handy for putting the car on the trailer — and a goodly number of jobs which might otherwise need a lot of muscle.

Hoist
A small one. Not essential, but handy — and compact enough to keep in the bottom of your tool box.

Rags
Cheap item this; take lots of them.

Tow rope

Very useful indeed. You can use old seat belt webbing. We use this flourescent nylon rope which threads into itself . . . but then we're flash.

Aluminium tape

Racer tape. Very strong and heat resistant, also very expensive. Something else we have used is film cameramen's tape. Something of the sort is invaluable.

Tool set

I've never been sorry that I bought the biggest and best-made cantilever tool box in the shop. It's very tough, doesn't flex at all when open, is heavily jointed rather than pop-rivetted, and holds everything I need.

Apart, obviously, from a hacksaw, screwdrivers, open-ended spanners, ring spanners, scissors, Stanley knife, pliers, Mole wrenches (two), a tyre pressure gauge, a plug gap tool and numerous odd nuts and bolts, springs, grommets and washers, it also holds two sets of spare spark plugs, points, condenser and a spare fanbelt.

Fire extinguisher

This is a tiny one. Not too much use. Our proper one was on the car when I took the photo, but I don't mind having a small one in my tool box as well.

Shoe white

For painting race numbers, dial-in times and rude words on the windows. Useful for cleaning white shoes, too.

Lubricating oil aerosol

WD40, Plus Gas — that sort of thing. Handy stuff anywhere.

This is the majority of our keep-racing-and-get-home-in-one-piece basic kit. It's usually augmented by Dennis' electronic tuning gauge, his very useful electrical trouble-shooting unit, another petrol can, the trolley jack and at least one other socket set so that two people can work on the car without having to poach tools from each other. Also, don't forget the necessities for man as well as machine – food and drink.

Brake fluid
Enough for both clutch and brake systems — twice. Also auto transmission fluid where appropriate.

Helmet
All present and correct and such as meets the appropriate BS 2495-77 and fits.

RAC racers' licence
Stating the obvious, but the number of experienced racers who forget it!

Wheelbrace
Good and strong and affording maximum leverage (minimum effort).

Foot pump
For adjusting slick pressures. Without one it's easy to let air out, more difficult to put air in.

Compression tester
Far from essential, but very useful, along with an electrical testing rig, for trouble-shooting.

Cordless electric drill
They're not that powerful, but do have their uses. We've got one, so we take it with us.

Trolley jack
An ordinary jack will do, but once you've discovered the speed and convenience of a trolley jack you'll not want any other. Add the axle stands to the lists, too, if you are going to be crawling under the car; absolutely essential.

Bourbon
Our favourite brand . . . to celebrate our victories, of course (note bottle is still full).

Seriously, though, as they say, don't forget your creature comforts completely. We tend to prey on other racers' ladies for butties or else queue up for deathburgers, but we do always take a good supply of beer (not for the driver), fresh orange juice and a huge vacuum flask of tea or coffee — either 1 litre or 1½ litres. Can't survive — let alone function well — without it. Plus Yorkies for Dennis and extra strong mints for me. Shame the groupies are so lax about chip butties and Marmite toast, though.

RACING YOUR CUSTOM MACHINE

Drag racing is very big in Britain and Sweden, and is growing slowly on the continent of Europe; but there's no doubt at all that customizing is bigger. Customizing and dragging have always been very close, with a lot of heritage in common. Find the customizer who isn't interested in dragging and you'll have found an exception. Yet only rarely do customizers stray on to the strip. One reason for this could well be the apparent insularity of the racers and race promoters; but that really is a case of one guy being stuck deep in his own field — like a race crew frantically stripping an engine in the pits while sticky-fingered members of the public crowd round and look on, gawping helplessly. The far more likely reason, though, is a fear on the part of the customizer, coupled with a little ignorance; he doesn't know what might happen to his car once out on the strip, and, crucially, he's afraid of finding out.

Many guys customize their machines and include performance on their priority list; be the emphasis on bodywork, paint, interior work, or whatever, very few leave their motors absolutely stock. We may only be talking about an initial process of prettifying; but almost inevitably that leads to engine reworking and transplanting later. There's no way the customizer can escape it, the mags are full of go-faster features, and full of derision for the puny. It's an element which matters little to the show-only custom machine, but there are truly very few of those in Europe. Most rods and custom machines see action — frequent action at that — on the streets, and that's the acid test. Tootling along wearing a super trick paint job is all very well, provided you don't mind being put in your place by the first gin-and-tonic drinker who happens along in his TR6.

Hence, although so many machines end up with at least half-decent mills, and although so many customizers adopt the current street racer fashion for their cars, very few actually end up on the quarter-mile.

It is certainly understandable that the rodder or customizer should not want to risk damage to his machine, but it has got to be true to say that any car is in greater danger on the public highway than on the drag strip. Be that danger to the paintwork from dust and stones, to bodywork from idle collisions and careless parkers, or to the engine and drivetrain from sheer exertion, you are a lot safer on the strip — where there is only one other car, and he's going in the same direction at the same sort of speed a fixed distance away from you — on the first two counts, and safe to much the same degree on the last point. Few people blow their motors up while dragging; and the vast majority of those that do are pilots of top cars, running exotic fuels and coaxing the mills to more than 10,000 revs. If your car has not been built really well it is as likely to crack up on the street as on the strip — and don't tell me that you *never* use its available power away from the lights or to get round trucks that are taking root. If it has been built well, then you really have very little to fear, and if I could choose a place for my car to break down while I was trying it out, I'd far rather a drag strip where there is help, expert advice and friends to lend a hand or tow me

home, than a country lane late on a Sunday night miles from home when I know I need to be out and about first thing in the morning.

To a very large degree you can anticipate trouble when weighing up whether or not your car is suitable for dragging. Assuming it to be in basically sound condition — able to fly through an MoT test — I would look at the engine and the drivetrain as two separate entities. Is the mill torquey? Does it rev quickly and easily? Does it breathe well? When you jab the accelerator do the revs whizz up quickly and cleanly as you press down? And fall back without any fuss when the pedal is released? Is the oil pressure up to scratch? Are the oil and the oil filter fairly recent and in good condition? You don't *need* to take the engine to its limits when dragging, and if you are confident that it can cope with a good blast away from the traffic lights on the High Street, then you really should be okay coming away from the christmas tree.

Now let's start on the drivetrain. See how good the clutch is. Is the action positive and the pedal firm? If the clutch parts are old and you haven't even

Dave Jones races this clean Mark 1 Consul at New York from time to time. The canary-yellow car is 3½-litre Rover-powered and turns in very respectable times.

STREET GASSER

XLV 555

This high-stepping Vauxhall has been built with street rather than strip in mind, I suspect, and was a frequent exhibit in raceway custom parades before the owner decided that street plus strip would be more fun.

looked at the hydraulic seals and the state of the fluid, then forget it. A recently and well-installed clutch will cause you no problems, and you'll find out with experience that the amount of wear it gets in an afternoon's dragging is probably less than if you'd spent the day crawling round town looking for parking spaces and ladies with big whatsits.

The gearbox. Is it basically sound? A negative approach here; if it's notchy or noisy then don't go dragging. A good shifter is as important as a good box, so the same thoughts apply. If you have transplanted the engine, the important consideration is that the gearbox and the rear axle are up to, or surpass, the stock load of the engine. In short, if you're going to put a 3-litre V6 in your Escort, then it makes a lot of sense to get a gearbox (manual or automatic) which was originally designed to cope with the sort of power a V6 will put out. Anything less will end in tears. Similarly, the back axle needs to be as tough — so in this case you're looking for one from a 3-litre Capri, a Zodiac, or a Granada. It'll need shortening, but it'll be right. This train of thought makes sense for the street, of course, but will stand you in good stead if you later decide to indulge in a little dragging (as well as ironing out problems like rear axle ratios straight away).

Having decided — or been reassured by this book — that your ace custom isn't going to fall apart rolling into stage, the next step might well be a little late-night checkout with a stopwatch. Before I went racing for the first time I drove out to a well-known and ever-deserted strip of country lane which runs dead straight for about three-quarters of a mile, without junctions or houses. Measure out as near to a quarter-mile as you can, and then try accelerating along it from rest, your mate timing you on the whizzo digital watch he got for Christmas. Not banzai stuff, this; it's a learning process. To have some idea — to within a half-second or so either way — of your car's potential times will be a great help; you'll know what you can take on and what to leave alone. Minor improvements — such as trying without the air filter, or the filter cartridge — can be tried at this stage. Other problems — such as flat spots, fuel starvation, or misfires — will also become apparent. The most important advantage, though, is to learn start-line technique. That's where the majority of races are won or lost. Folk tend to over-react

— drop the clutch and stamp on the gas — and usually end up bogging the mill. Take it easy and sure and keep away from the dramatic stuff — all that tyre-squealing and those smokey burnouts are for the future. If you don't learn a lot about your car and how to make it honk, then you've not got a future in dragging.

As for the right meeting to start at, you've got two choices; Production or

Take care with tall screens and hope the scrutineer lets you race without a roll-cage, but there's no reason why rods shouldn't go dragging. Owner Andy Parfitt was certainly determined to try his hand.

The final of the 1980 Street Racing Championship and Dave Holmes in the 350-ci Chevy-powered Ventora steals the crucial early lead on Bill Sherratt's Tiger and went on to take the title. True street machines on the quarter-mile make for great entertainment.

129

Street class racing, or bracket racing. Production is very unlikely, so if you go for class racing expect to race in Street. A better option by far at this stage is bracket racing. Never wanting to make a fool of myself, I'd go for a modest bracket meeting every time. In bracket racing you can survive by consistency rather than speed; you need not run at full bore. If you can run consistent times and place yourself at the top end of a lowly bracket then you stand a very good chance of coming away with a prize. All the details have been dealt with in our chapter on getting started in the drags.

There really is very little restriction on what you can race. Lowriders can cut it, so can rods — though you'd be advised to remove tall screens from T-buckets and the like. A static custom show is all very well, but it does deny you the chance to show off an important dimension of your car. So often you hear folk in the crowds at custom shows pointing and telling each other that they bet it never sees the street. Prove them wrong by taking it not only to the street — but to the strip as well. I started The Street Racing Championship in 1979 with exactly this in mind; let the custom guys show how their motors really run. Winning awards for custom shows is quite a blast, but just wait for the thrill of driving home from the strip with a winner-of-bracket trophy on the back shelf. You know it makes sense.

Taking the Strain

SPONSORSHIP

Sponsorship is advertising; your car is your billboard, and in return for cash or goods you write a supplier's name on the side, or perhaps just display his product's sticker. The size of the advert is obviously related to its value.

When it comes to sponsorship, drag racing is very much a poor relation among motor sports. Go to any circuit and you'll find a paying sponsor's name or logo everywhere you look — on the track sides, on participants' clothing, on race cars and every kind of support vehicles, and even down the legs of the ladies who form the start-line cheer-leaders. The top leagues in dragging are almost invariably sponsored in some way or other, but never to a really generous degree, and sponsorship spreads downwards less often than one would think. The fault can lie with no-one but the racer — it's up to him to go and persuade a businessman to sponsor him, and to approach any potential sponsor in a realistic, informed and professional manner. It's rare for a drag racer not to moan, at least occasionally, that he could do so much better if he only had more money to spend on the car; the fact of the matter is that the money is probably there for the asking.

As a generalization it is better to go looking for one major sponsor than half a dozen smaller ones. It is as easy to ask someone for £2,000 as it is to ask them for £500; the amount of work involved on your part is the same, and of course, you only have to do it once (for each successful application). This means that for major sponsorship you could be looking to large national companies, perhaps, as opposed to a local business. Not a bad idea as the bigger company will have a larger promotional budget to dip into and, with more potential customers, may well feel that he stands to get more out of such a deal.

Another advantage of a single large sponsor is the fact that you will then have only one name or slogan or logo to fit on to the side of the car. Imagine having a different name on each body panel, each in that company's colours — the words would get too small to be effectively read by folk in the crowd and your car could well end up looking like a carnival float. Also, you've only got one set of people to keep happy — a sponsorship deal is only just beginning when the cash is handed over; but more of that later.

An important point to decide on is exactly what you want from a sponsor, and this will depend to some degree on the level at which you are racing.

Years back, when I made an abortive start in dragging, I negotiated with a local garage owner to write the name of his business on my bracket racer in return for evening access to his fully equipped workshop, and for routine parts at trade prices. If you're on good terms with a local garage then that is a very easy deal to strike, and while you are hardly taking anything at all from him, the advantages to a low-buck bracket or Street/Production outfit are obvious.

Thus, sponsorship need not be cash — it can be products or even services (I know someone who had a sponsor who had nothing to do with the race car, but earned his space on the boot lid by providing the tow car and trailer every weekend). Trade prices on items such as oil and plugs and speed

Don 'The Snake' Prudhomme, like all the top US Funny Car pilots, is heavily sponsored and in his case the largest single sponsor is the American Army. Would you have thought of approaching say, the RAF for a deal?

equipment will, roughly speaking, be about half retail, so if you are approaching a local accessory or goodies shop, the value of such parts to you might be £300 in a season, but only cost your sponsor £150. You can both come out of such an arrangement with a very good deal.

In the main, and with cars in higher classes, cash is more useful than goods, and asking a big company for funds is not easy. For one thing you wouldn't believe the number of approaches a company will receive, some ill-thought-out, many silly, and others to further good causes, but of little use to the company involved.

The next decision is whom to approach. Avoid obvious no-nos; a motor manufacturer is unlikely to sponsor a car with a body which is their own but out of date — let alone someone else's. The sponsor is only going to be interested in a car which can be identified with his product. Roof rack manufacturers and people selling fuel economy are unlikely to like you.

Sponsorship money will have to come from somewhere within a company, and that place will be their promotional or advertising budget. Companies which spend a lot of money on advertising, especially in 'youth market' areas and the custom/young motoring realms, are favourites. Buy a few magazines and do a little homework.

Nor need you restrict yourself to companies involved in the motor trade. Magazines sponsor dragging — as do construction companies, ferry lines, insurance companies, radio stations, jeans manufacturers and cigarette companies.

So, having decided that Almost Circular Wheels or Spark Shark Electronic Ignition Ltd might be worth approaching, what's the next step? Well, you don't just get on the 'phone. You've got to present them with a formal proposal; including pictures it would be about 10 pages long. Get one of those A4 glossy folders where the sheets slip down into transparent plastic envelopes to form the pages. Then fill it with nicely typed pages of information; neat and clean and without mistakes.

The point of the folder is that it looks good and will make a better impression than a few notes on the back of an envelope. Smartness in presentation reflects well on your race team; people assume that professional proposals come from professionals. The file will be passed, doubtless, from hand to hand while a decision is being made, and needs to stay clean and legible. Protect yourself now against the spilt coffee of the future.

Bribe a friendly secretary to type it up (on a good machine) and lay it out. Don't type on both sides of the paper, and leave 1½ spaces between each line. The title page might just read:

THE 'YOUR NAME' DRAG RACE TEAM

A sponsorship proposal which could take your product name into a young and most exciting area of motor sport for a very small outlay.

Presented by:

then add your name and address, phone numbers and the date. Leave the title page clean and start the meat on page 2.

You cannot assume that Almost Circular Wheels will know exactly what drag racing is all about. Start by explaining the sport — briefly. Tell them how exciting it is and how faithful the fans are. Then tell them why you think the sport could be of commercial interest to them. Almost Circular Wheels spend fortunes selling to the custom crowd, fine; tell them how closely related are dragging and customizing. Give them the figures for attendance at drag strips, and back that up with figures for the major custom shows, and the readership figures for the national custom mags — all of which interest themselves with drag racing. Statistics are terrific, so do some research and then quote like mad (at the moment the four glossy custom mags have an audited total sale of half a million copies every month, for example, the *National Custom Car Show* has seen attendances of 128,000 and the figure for the *Rod and Custom Show* is usually around 85,000).

The point which you are making from all this is that you will not only race the car, but will exhibit it at the larger custom shows, and try and get it featured in at least one of the magazines. Hence: 20 race meetings with an average of 12,000 people, plus 250,000 people at five or six shows, and features in two magazines selling a total of 210,000 copies . . . gosh, the ACW-sponsored drag car is being seen by 700,000 people in one season. Now, for even the most hard-bitten promotional manager, that's a healthy figure — and every single one of those people is a potential customer of ACW.

Go on to tell them that you could, of course, paint the car in ACW's colours, and would add their name to the car's name — so that it would be referred to in show programmes and over raceway PAs as 'The ACW Thunderer' — thus adding on a bit more promotion for them, and outline exactly how big their name and logo would be on the car.

Add that the car would naturally be made available for the sponsors, should they have a press day, and for photographs for the sponsor to use in his ads or whatever. Then give your price. A very short budget, explaining where the money will go is a good idea — especially stressing improvements. And make it a round figure, and realistic.

A brief biography of yourself and/or the driver is helpful — and don't be afraid to stress anything which might make you stand out from other sponsorship applications; experience, the fact that you are a woman (where applicable), that you're a peer or are registered as disabled — whatever.

Big photos of the car are vital — and an artist's impression of what it might look like with the prospective sponsor's name and logo on the side might be a useful luxury if you've got any friends who are artists or draughtsmen.

The temptation is to send the glistening prospectus straight off to ACW at this point. If you do, enclose a brief covering letter, asking very politely if ACW would be kind enough to read the enclosed. It is probably a better idea to write to ACW and a dozen other companies first, asking them if they would care to read your proposal.

Getting to the right man is a very good start. In a smaller company it would be someone in a post such as General Manager, while in a big national company there would be a promotions department with a Promotions Manager. If you're not sure then get on the 'phone and simply ask the girl on ACW's switchboard for the man's name — may take a minute if their departments go by trendier names — and check that you have the full address of the head office.

Once you are sponsored and your 'ACW Thunderer' makes its debut, you are a representative of that company just as if you were on their payroll. Never do anything at all to bring their name into disrepute, never criticise their products, and sew their badges on to your overalls and display their stickers on your support car. ACW are paying you for a service, and the more you do for them, the more likely they are to give you another cheque next year, and the more likely it will be that other companies will want to get in on the act, too.

So, go and find the race commentator, tell him about your sponsor and ask if he'll give a few mentions over the PA; race commentators tend to be very appreciative of such requests. Tell your local newspaper and talk them into doing one of those 'local lad' features. Why not an interview on your local radio station — in their motoring spot or general news magazine? And if you've got any news at all — a win, a prize from a show, a new class or strip record — let everyone know. Write a little press release for the magazines and, most importantly, send them a good-quality photograph; a good burnout or wheelie shot will almost certainly get published in the news section. Many big companies have their own publicity agents who will do this for you once you've established contact.

Going back to the magazines for a moment, don't be frightened of them. They appreciate that the sport needs increased sponsorship money, and should be only too glad to give you a mention. Don't get too pushy with them, though (as a race of beings, journalists get huffed easily), and don't buttonhole the journalists at the track — they're too busy. A cheery wave and a genial hello will help you a lot more . . . then 'phone them with the news of your win later in the week.

Keep a scrapbook. Hang on to every mention you get in a paper or mag, and list every meeting or show you've attended and note anything of interest. At the end of the year show this to your sponsor. If you do a lot of winning you'll be on the strip longer and more likely to be mentioned in the mags, but just being there and putting on a good show is what your sponsor is paying good money for . . . and now, to make the most of that, read the chapters on team identity and showmanship.

Dream Teams and Clean Machines

TEAM IDENTITY

Some of those amongst us, having seen 'Two Lane Blacktop' maybe, don't reckon too much to all this team business. The image of the archetypal bracket bandit is some cool dude in tight jeans and white T-shirt — cigarette pack folded under one sleeve — wearing mirrored shades and a big cowboy hat pulled low over his forehead; he chews on a match and talks in grunts — nyuhuh?

Smashing. But when he does speak he has to use his broad Brighouse and Rastrick accent — more trans-M62 than Mid-West, and that ruins the effect.

Or, as a friend's young daughter said to me, having seen John Mills lolling moodily by his Roadrunner: 'Is that man American?' 'No', I said, 'He comes from Stockport.' She sounded confused: 'But he's wearing an American hat.'

As an extension of showmanship a good team image can be very important. Some people simply don't want to be all dressed up in Andy Pandy suits with their team name written on the back; it's purely personal preference. There again, it does look smart and professional, and certainly helps the crowd with its loyalties.

If you have a single major sponsor I would consider it only courteous to sport his badges on your overalls, and because you could be considered his 'works team' all those overalls should match. It will certainly help in some situations to be immediately identifiable as a team member. For much the same reasons most strips provide smart and bright uniforms for their officials, marshals and start-line crew.

Some teams run to overalls and jackets which match the colour scheme of the race car, have its name and logo emblazoned on their backs and breast pockets, and also have their names and jobs — driver, mechanic, team manager, or whatever — on their T-shirts. The theme flows through the team, as it were, and they never fail to look impressive.

Such an approach is very important if you are looking to any direct commercial spin-off from your racing. A very small number of top racers are wise enough to run a race team fan club, or sell T-shirts or other bits and pieces with their car and name well displayed. The international paragon of such commercialism — and crowd identification — is The Blue Max Team (who earn themselves a considerable amount of money from their own success and popularity).

The team livery can, of course, be carried a stage further — on to support car and trailer. Paint them all so that they match; indeed, the sides of the support car can be regarded as second-division billboard space when you are getting sponsorship.

Support cars are worth a word or two. They need to be reliable, long legged, as comfortable as you can afford, and very large indeed. You can never have too much room in your support car. For this reason, large American estate cars are always popular, as are Range Rovers, big vans and the larger American pickups (especially with demountable tops) and 4WD vehicles such as Chevy Blazers. Half a dozen racers run buses — really —

with ramps so that the car or bikes can be run up into the back, and then lots of living and sleeping space and storage areas up front. Expensive to run, but they make a lot of sense for the really serious racer.

Ramp-backed trucks with crew cabs — such as the AA relay use — or a larger American equivalent, must be just about ideal, but at the lower end of the business the best thing you can lay your hands on is a large, cheap and uncomplicated estate car such as a Granada. We've never yet had a big enough support car, but then, the more space you have, the more friends

Ian Lloyd's super little Topolino C/A is a well presented and tastefully painted car which is worthy of a feature in any custom magazine.

How a Swedish team go racing. This huge box trailer is pulled by a long-wheelbase crew-cab pickup, with a tool store on the bed. Note how the sponsor's name is well displayed.

seem to drop in to share your butties in the lunch break.

Over-fussy and over-intricate paint schemes are for custom shows, not for drag cars. Bold, contrasting colours in simple straightforward designs invariably look much better on a race car. And keep well away from anyone else's livery; the object of the exercise is to have an individual and instantly recognizable racer. The acid test is how will the car looks in a photo — and, indeed, in a black-and-white photo; which brings you into the art school world of tone, line, hue and form. The majority of pictures in the magazines

A very fast and equally good looking car that's always well presented is Dave Warne's 437 Chevy-powered Vega estate, which is justifiably popular with the crowd and the press.

are in black-and-white (colour pix tend to 'run' larger and there are then fewer of them). Regardless of what times the car is running — the one which looks sharp and dramatic is going to be the one which gets into print; art editors stay in their offices and don't give a damn who won what.

On the other hand, if you're making this wild grabbing paint job stand up on its back legs, or performing similar eye-catching antics, you will come in for even more attention . . . which brings us neatly to showmanship.

SHOWMANSHIP

One does wonder sometimes just how many drag racers are even aware of the crowds of spectators, the thousands of pairs of eyes studying their every move. Driving any class of racer makes total concentration vital; the car, the lights and the opposition all need attention and coming down to the start-line a driver will be psyching himself up hard for the imminent race.

So it takes a special sort of racer who can bring the crowd into his consciousness at such moments. In the theatre, among actors, they call it 'playing to the gallery'. It's showmanship, and the guys who go out of their way to entertain and thrill the crowd are adding a fuller dimension to the sport, and — as the shrewd will realize — are bound to be greatly repaid by spectator support. The crowd adore showmen — so do the guys from the press — and in the long run it can do you (and your sponsors) nothing but good.

The other side of this particular coin is that anything which could be seen as delinquency or plain messing about will upset the start marshals and officials and may put you out of competition for one reason or another. Best be on the safe side and let the start marshals in on any start-line practical jokes.

If you want to make a bit of a name for yourself the most important thing to do is to win; that always impresses the crowd. Not everyone can win, though, and simply making a good showing — turning up with a good-looking car, a well turned out crew, and being seen to be trying hard — will also impress both the crowd and the media. Monstrous burnouts and pulling wheelies off the line will also make a happy impression on the spectators and the press men.

Big burnouts are no problem. You may need to apply water, or a compound such as Redex to produce really impressive clouds of smoke, but the process is to switch on the Line-Loc and then just let the power through. Beware the car whipping sideways and beware breaking things — rear axles in general and half-shafts in particular are especially prone to cracking up during heavy burnouts. Super showmen get silly and go in for champagne burnouts.

You need a lot of horsepower to manage a rolling burnout, fueller-style, but a mechanical style of Line-Loc, working like a conventional handbrake so that you can ease the braking off the front wheels, could help a Street or Production lay smoking rubber right across the line. Do so and you can be certain that from then on all eyes will be on you, not your opponent; and — importantly — *he'll* know it.

Very occasionally, top fuellers and funny cars go in for full flame burnouts, where petrol is poured on to the track behind the start-line and is deliberately set alight. Jolly dramatic it looks, too, and at night it's just unbelievable.

About 15 years ago Hurst built a demo burnout car based on an Oldsmobile 4-4-2. Fitted with *two* blown and injected 432 motors — one at the back and one at the front — this almost unbelievable car ran rolling

Now that's a real burnout! You'll have to take my word that there's a Pontiac Tempest in there somewhere.

A full flame burnout on a winter's evening at Santa Pod Raceway. All the business from Highway Patrol.

burnouts with all four wheels smoking. Nutty as hell, but what a performer!

Pulling wheelies away from the lights must rate alongside the practice of allowing cars to slither sideways towards the barrier during rolling burnouts, in terms of drawing *Ooohs* and *Aaahs* from the paying public. Some guys, like Al O'Connor, are famous for it. A car which is sitting up on its back legs is not easily controlled, and is certainly not going to run as fast as it would with all four on the floor, but gosh it does look amazing, 'specially when the wheelie bars (which come out from the back of a car to limit how far back it goes when wheelie-ing) start sparking on the track.

Demon biker Pip Higham is much loved for the enormous wheelies he pulls. Given a bye run, most folk just tootle down the strip in their own good time, but at Santa Pod on one occasion Pip was about to run a bye and

Al O'Connor in the much appreciated Al's Gasser reaches for the skies. These antics have led to more than one wreck.

decided that as everyone was looking at him he ought to keep them entertained. He wheelied so hard that the bike started drifting right out of shape and he actually crossed the centre-line and so disqualified himself. It takes a showman to lose a bye run.

Special demonstration wheelie cars are very popular with drag promoters. They are constructed for the sole purpose of blatting down the quarter-mile with their front wheels way up in the air. Britain's first wheelie car was built by Roy Phelps at Santa Pod Raceway in the Sixties. It was based on a Corvette Stingray bodyshell. There have been a couple of others over here,

This is Roy Phelps in the Stingray, and although this Mike Key photo was taken some years ago the car re-appeared at the SPR Brighton show in 1980.

Dave Smith rides special demonstration runs for Pennine and this is just one of his tricks. Dave holds the world wheelie record with a distance of more than 17 miles as I write this.

but the only one running at the moment is the ex-NDRC Vauxhall estate car which runs at Pennine's New York Raceway. Powered by an Oldsmobile 455 located behind the back axle, and steering by independent brakes on the rear wheels, the driver has to look through Perspex panels between the front wheels to see where he or she is going. Accelerating hard and running at a 45-degree angle to the rest of the world, a wheelie car never fails to delight. Just wait for side-by-side wheelie racing.

Raceway promoters are also very fond of thrust-powered cars, and nothing produces quite so much crowd reaction as a jet or rocket car. Most jet or rocket cars are built for deadly serious attempts on records and perform demonstration runs as a publicity-gaining sideline. Barry Bowles built the peroxide-powered rocket car The Blonde Bombshell and made demo runs with that before the car was involved in a terminal crash while aiming for a land speed record on Pendine Sands, in Wales.

Malcolm Olley's jet car was a frequent visitor to British strips at much the same time. To stand near the car on take-off is quite an experience, the noise building up to a skull-splitting whine before the machine roars off in a blast of dust and debris, usually blowing the start-line timing equipment away with the force.

Both home-grown cars were eclipsed in '78 and '79 when Sammy Miller came to Santa Pod with his Vanishing Point rocket car. Looking deceptively like a conventional Funny Car, Slammin' Sammy staggered everyone with his first appearance on September 17, 1978. The peroxide rocket was producing 5,000 lb of thrust, and hurtled Sammy to times of 4.41 seconds

Getting a touch out of shape and heading towards the Armco, SPR's little truck pickup wheelie machine echoes American demo vehicles.

at 290.6 mph. No-one had ever seen anything quite like that in Europe. Three weeks previously, Sammy had run the car in Sweden and managed a best time there of 4.79/228; Europe's first ever 4-second pass. On July 8, 1979 Sammy brought Vanishing Point out at SPR again. Determined to top 300 mph, Sammy finished his fourth run with a time of 4.20 seconds at 307.6 mph. Later in that year, though, Vanishing Point was written off when Sammy ran out of shutdown area at SPR. Doubtless his European record will stand until he comes back with a new projectile.

Big rigs have put in regular appearances at Pennine's New York strip ever since Europe's first truck dragging field was arrayed there on August 20, 1978. The rigs tend to run quarter-mile times between 20 and 23 seconds, with terminal speeds between 55 and 60 mph. The trucks are not always

Malcolm Olley's jet car at Long Marston. As the power-plant reaches maximum potential just before take-off the whine becomes truly skull-splitting. Have you ever stood next to a Boeing?

Truck racing has been popular in the States for some years and is appropriately well advanced there. These big-bonneted rigs look good on the quarter-mile.

Clerk of the Course Tony Murray looks after his own as Mr Robey burns out in his Transcon prior to a run.

particularly popular with the other racers, but do delight the crowds and, in their way, do expand drag racing's horizons.

Europe's first demonstration dragging truck appeared at New York in 1979. The Bandag Bullet has never turned in truly shattering times, but has topped 100 mph with ease over the flying-mile. The Bullet does come into a category of vehicles, though, where times are not too relevant; the point is not competition, but the all-important entertainment of the paying public; 'playing to the gallery' certainly brings them back for more.

Based on an A-Series Ford, the Bandag Bullet made quite a splash for all concerned, and especially the commercial tyre-producing sponsors, when it made its debut.

DRAGGING IN EUROPE

Sweden

Interest in customizing and drag racing has been very great in Sweden since the mid-Sixties, though punitive type approval legislation keeps the former under very strict control. Their major custom and dragging magazine, *Start & Speed,* was founded in 1965 and the first full drag meeting was held at the Scandinavian Raceway at Anderstorp in 1968. The sport has not had an easy life to date — even in such a sparsely populated country there is always someone to complain about the noise or the traffic congestion. Anyone who has seen the Swedes racing in the UK, though, will appreciate just how seriously they take their drag racing and how well they turn out their cars.

Their success is built on a solid basis of ability and big finance. For various reasons they've got their communal act together better than anyone else in Europe and have attracted sponsorship on an impressive scale. Anders Hasselstrom, for example, is sponsored by the Swedish Air Force — for a sum which, reputedly, would run into five figures in sterling.

The Swedes do have a good number of their own performance shops, but given the cash resources, do tend to buy top cars in from the States. And when you're working at that level you can be certain of getting value — and fast reliable times — for your money. Sweden can also boast a large and rapid contingent of Street cars; a fact due, in some part, I imagine, both to larger investment (again) and the happy fact that they are blessed with so much basic heavy Detroit metal from which they can start.

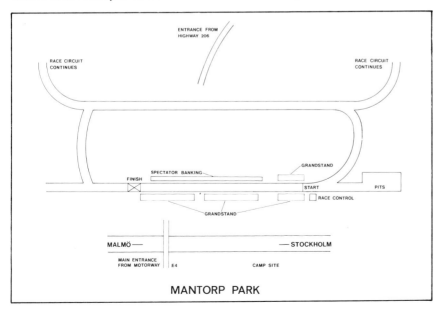

MANTORP PARK

There's always a danger of underselling the Swedes, but see them at SPR, or on their home ground as here, and you soon realize just how professional, and quick, they are.

A brace of custom-painted Volvos ready to run at Mantorp Park, with Kenneth Leander's car on the left and Lars Magnusson's on the right.

The sport is organized through 40 or so local clubs, which are affiliated to the Swedish Hot Rod Association (each locally named; so, SHRA-Göteborg or SHRA-Stockholm). The capital's club, unsurprisingly, is the largest.

Sweden currently has one permanent strip — Mantorp Park, between Mjölby and Linköping, south-west of Stockholm. There is a strong possibility, though, that the Scandinavian Raceway, which is about 80 miles south-east of Göteborg, will also become a permanent venue in the near

The mainland Europeans are equally enthusiastic bikers. This is Conny Riklund smoking home on his 1,080-cc Honda.

future, sharing its facilities with other motor sports.

There are eight other venues, all airports which are occasionally occupied by the racers for a day's dragging. Working south they are: Piteå Dragway, Hallviken Airport, Sollefteå Airport, Hälsingerakan, Orsa Dragway, Johannisberg Airport, Emmaboda Airport and Bulltofta. An average Swedish season keeps fairly strictly to the summer months, but will include between 15 and 20 meetings. Addresses:

SHRA-Stockholm
Kampementsgatan 4
115 38 Stockholm
Sweden.

Södra Stockholm Drag Racers Club
Dalkärrsvägen 11
14600 Tullinge
Stockholm
Sweden.

Finland, Norway, Denmark.

The rest of Scandinavia does rather operate in Sweden's shadow. There are a few race meetings at *ad hoc* strips in Finland, but despite the absence of any sort of full racing programme the national clubs proliferate — especially, I'm told, in Norway.

Danish Hot Rod Association
Jörn Duelund
Svinget 4
2300 S Köpenhamm
Denmark.

American Car Club
Svein Myhre
Postboks 1177
7001 Trondheim
Norway.

Finnish Hot Rod Association
Box 7
00601 Helsingfors 60
Finland.

American Car Club — Southern Norway
Postboks 27
Simensbråten
Oslo 11
Norway.

Netherlands

Drag racing in Holland is run by AMSC Explosion, and their biggest event is the annual bike-only meeting which is held at Drachten — on the factory airfield of Phillips. Drachten is in Friesland, in northern Holland, 10 miles south-east of Leeuwarden and about 20 miles west of Groningen.

Algemene Motor Sprint Club
A Kempvink
Ijweg 1061
Hoofdoorp
Holland.

West Germany

German dragging has always owed much to the presence of American servicemen and their machinery; there have been well-organized service drag clubs and display teams in Germany for more than 15 years. The largest native club is the 1 DVD.

1 Deutscher Verein Fur Dragracing EV
Felgenstrasse 11
6456 Langenselboede
Germany.
President: Hans Klaoss.

The US service drag clubs include the Hanau Auto Club, which has an air base strip outside the town of the same name, 15 miles east of Frankfurt. There is a similar set-up at Mainz-Finten, which is much the same distance to the west of Frankfurt, on the Rhine. This venue does have its problems, though — notably a lack of security against those intent on coming in through the perimeter fences — it seems that the air strip at Kassel, nearby, will be the venue for German dragging interest in the future.

France

Drag racing had been making cautious inroads in La Belle France for some time before it surfaced with a vengeance at Le Mans in 1980. Racing there

Drag racing comes to France. Here is Ronnie Picardo on the move at Le Mans and just letting go of the 'chute.

was held over an eighth-mile strip and the experiment was repeated in 1981 for a crowd of around 65,000 people. The same year there was also the first of what could well become a regular series at Circuit Paul Ricard, near Le Beusseut, north of Toulon. Again racing over an eighth, 33,000 people attended — and that was out of season. The racers were almost all Swedes and Britons and they were well pleased with their trips to France — particularly as the prize money was realistic. The French are certainly taking the sport to their heart and are building race cars of their own. The evidence suggests that these will mostly be Modified, with a few fuellers.

I know of no French drag clubs at present, though doubtless they are emerging. The best contact for the sport in that country for the time being is probably the magazine which was heavily involved in the racing both at Le Mans and Paul Ricard:

Two fuellers race down the eighth-of-a-mile strip at Le Mans before a huge crowd at the course more famous for 24-hour enduros.

Chrome & Flames
95 Rue de la Boetie
75008 Paris
France.

Drag Dictionary

JARGON EXPLAINED

Bleach box
Area of the strip, usually just back from the start-line, which is reserved for burnouts. Water is applied to the track just in front of the rear slicks. Bleach is no longer allowed though.

Blower
A supercharger. Engine-driven, it sits on top, or occasionally on the side of the engine, and forces the fuel vapour/air mixture into the engine under increased pressure.

A blower sitting above the stock V6 of a Street class Ford Granada.

Break out
To exceed one's qualifying time, either at all, or by a set limit. Breaking out disqualifies you.

Bug catcher
The 3-port or 4-port manifold which sits above the blower casing on most blown engines.

Bump spot
The slowest qualifying car in an elimination field. An uneasy place to be.

Burnout
Getting the rear slicks to spin while keeping the car more or less stationary. The friction burns a layer of rubber off the slicks, cleaning them of grit and damage, and also heating the rubber so that — soft and sticky — they grip the track better. Water will be used to help break the natural traction and avoid breakages in the car's drivetrain.

Butterflies
(a) The vents over the ports on a bug catcher. (b) What a driver may feel in his tummy as he comes into stage.

Bye
If there is an odd number of cars in the eliminations, or if one of the competing cars breaks or fails to make it to the line for any reason, the other car will run alone. This is a bye run. Speed is unimportant on a bye run, but the run must be completed (without external help; the racer can push his car across the finish-line if need be), and the driver must not disqualify himself by red-lighting or crossing the centre-line.

Cherry
Picking a cherry, or lighting a cherry; switching on the disqualifying red light at the bottom of the christmas tree by leaving the line too soon.

Christmas tree
The start-line lights. Two sets of lights arranged vertically, one line for each lane; they help the racers get into stage and then show amber and green for go. The red light at the bottom is the disqualifier (see above).

Contingency money
A contingency fund is when a company or organization adds to the prize money of the meeting, on condition that the winning vehicle is displaying the company's product sticker. A very useful form of sponsorship, and mutually beneficial. Check with the strip's race secretary for details at each venue.

Cut-outs
Valves in the exhaust system which allow the silencers to be by-passed on a street car so that the exhaust gases exit direct from the headers. For strip use only.

Digger
A rear-engined rail. So called because of its nose-down 'digging-in' stance.

Digging in
A vague expression which indicates that a car is going down the strip well — getting lots of traction, its wheels not spinning uselessly, and keeping a straight course.

ET
Elapsed time. The time taken by the race car, bike or truck between cutting the beams of light at the start-line and the finish-line. Despite the emphasis given to ETs they do not decide the winner of a race; first across the line wins — and that is not always the guy with the better ET.

Elephant motor
Term used to describe the big cubic inch aluminium engines. Often taken to refer specifically to the Milodon engine.

Firewall
The bulkhead between engine and cockpit.

Flathead
An engine which has, but for a little finning, flat heads externally, due to its being a side-valve mill. Flatheads are the original Ford V8 design, very old-fashioned now, but do still retain a very enthusiastic crowd of fans (*eg* The British Flathead Racers Association).

Flopper
Old name for a Funny Car. The term was originally 'fender flopper', which reflected the extreme flimsiness of the glass-fibre bodies.

Fuel
Slang for nitro-methanol.

Fueller
A dragster running on fuel (see above).

Gas
Gas in the American sense, that is. Petrol, we call it.

Gasser
A race car running on gas (as above) rather than fuel.

Goat
Slang name for the Pontiac GTO, one of the great American muscle cars.

A Pontiac GTO, or Goat, representing sheer street/strip muscle. The black bits behind the wheels are shreds of rubber after a particularly heavy burnout.

Grudge racing
Grudge racing/needle racing/match racing; they all mean the same thing; races outside a meeting's programme where one racer simply challenges another racer, for whatever reason. Very bad form to refuse to race.

Headers
The exhaust manifold system. Headers comprise the complete exhaust system on all but a few Street class cars.

Headers. This is an interesting up-and-over style on the old Chicken Coupe Comp Altered. Note the fuel-injection set-up.

Hemi
An engine in which the top of the cylinder chamber is a completely smooth hemispherical shape. An optimum design for gas flow, it also allows the sparking plug to be located right at the top of the chamber.

Holeshot
The racer with really good reactions who launches from the line at the earliest possible moment without pulling a red light has 'scored a holeshot' over his opponent.

Iron motor
The classic Chrysler 392 Hemi engine; base of many a drag car.

This is what a beautifully turned out blown and injected Hemi engine looks like. The headers are the short type.

Jimmy

Slang for GMC, as in the make of blower. Although the term is used for all GMC blowers, a Jimmy is truly a purpose-built alloy-cased unit with teflon-tipped rotors and quick-change front ends.

Ladder bars

Rear axle locating bars which aid traction by reducing tramping and axle wind-up. (See Building chapter earlier.)

Laying rubber

The same as a rolling burnout — a burnout on the move, where a car or bike spins and smokes the slicks right across the line before coming back to stage. The racer will reverse carefully so that on take-off he will be driving along the thin strips of warm rubber which he has just laid.

Line-loc

An electrical device which locks up the front brakes only so that the rear wheels can rotate freely without the car moving for the duration of the burnout.

Lunch

To lunch an engine is to blow it up or seriously disable it — a verb interchangeable with 'grenade'. Lunch also means three deathly burgers with wet onions and two cans of tepid beer at midday.

Mill

Slang word; simply means engine.

Moon tank

Dean Moon made specialist racing equipment in the United States. His petrol tanks were distinctively barrel-shaped, round in section, and made of high-quality spun aluminium.

Pop

No reference to your old dad. If the fuel in a blown mill 'blows back' under power, the item liable to suffer damage is the blower; hence 'popping a blower'. To help avoid this, blowers are fitted with a heavily-sprung gas-escape plate called a pop-off valve.

A moon tank sitting up front on a Comp Altered and making a neat and tidy installation.

Out of shape
To come off the line and not be pointing in the right direction. A car with handling problems — veering to one side or whatever — is getting out of shape.

Big John's Mustang goes back a bit, but this shot captures him well out of shape on a heavily powered rolling burnout.

Quick-change rear
A rear axle set-up which allows the final ratios in the diff to be changed with far less than the usual amount of work — and with the axle still *in situ*. Very useful for turning a street muscle car into a competitive racer within minutes.

Rail
The traditional dragster, long, sparse and narrow, is called a rail.

Sandbagging
If a driver feels that he has won a race decisively, but is nervous of breaking out, he may brake hard just before the line to lower the recorded ET. This practice is called sandbagging.

Scatter shield
Usually comprising a flexible blanket of bullet-proof vest material which wraps around the transmission, the scatter shield protects racer and spectator alike should the gears or clutch explode. Can also be made of steel sheet.

SEMA specification
The Specialist Equipment Manufacturers Association is an American body which keeps a close watch on its own produce so that a sticker indicating that a part meets SEMA specification guarantees its quality.

Shifter
The gear lever.

Shutdown
If you beat your opponent in a drag race you have 'shut him down'.

Shutdown area
The run-off at the far end of the strip where cars slow down before turning back towards the pits via a return road.

Six-pack
Progressive carburation found on some late-Sixties Mopar muscle machinery. The six-pack consists of three twin-choke carbs. The car runs on the centre carb normally and the other two open progressively under heavy acceleration.

Slicks
Racing tyres for the driven wheels. They have a smooth tread, are made of soft rubber compound, and are used at low inflations. (See earlier chapters.)

Slingshot
An affectionate term for front-engined dragsters; usually older machines such as the Allard kit dragger of the mid-Sixties.

Slusher
Or slush box. Automatic transmission.

Stage
To be 'in stage' is to be correctly waiting, just breaking the first (rear) light beam on the start-line. When both cars are staged the christmas tree sequence will begin.

Street machine
A distinct but ill-defined American style of street/strip car; a much misapplied term over here. A street machine is a street racer — heavy metal built for street dragging and equally at home on the strip.

Street sleeper
A racer in disguise. Surprise is always a useful weapon, and if you appear to be driving a stock saloon with rusty bumpers and a roof rack then the impact will be all the greater when you thunder away under the power of that well-concealed 426 Hemi mill.

Tipping the can
Running a fueller with a high proportion of nitro to methanol. Also known as 'loading for bear' apparently.

T-bucket
A small replica Model T bodyshell, frequently seen on Competition Altereds.

Trick
A difficult word to define. One that is used to denote something which is pleasing to the eye of an appreciative expert — and used in all sorts of contexts, aesthetic or technical. A paint job can be trick, so can a fuel injection set-up. Especially true of anything new or innovative.

Turtle back
The short sloping boot-like protruberance often found covering the rear axle on a T-bucket-bodied car.

Wheelie
Lifting the car's front wheels clear of the tarmac. Not recommended for aerodynamics or handling, but wheelie experts are great favourites with the crowds. Some strips have special demonstration 'wheelie cars'. (See the chapter on showmanship.)

GUIDE TO CLUBS AND STRIPS

SANTA POD RACEWAY is Britain's largest drag venue. Its administration is handled by the British Drag Racing Association (BDRA), who can be contacted through:

Margaret Warne
(Competition Secretary)
149 Horseshoe Lane
Garston
Watford
Herftfordshire.
Tel: 09273-79354

or Ann Johnson
(Membership Secretary)
Unit 7, Pontiac Works
Fernbank Road
North Ascot
Berkshire.
Tel: 03447-3519 (daytime)

The strip is located on the borders of Bedfordshire and Northamptonshire, near the village of Podington. It can be reached by turning west off the A6 at Rushden, 13 miles north of Bedford, or by leaving the M1 at intersection 14 and then going through Newport Pagnell to join the A509, which will take you through Olney and Bozeat before SPR's own signposts indicate the strip itself (about 17 miles from the M1).

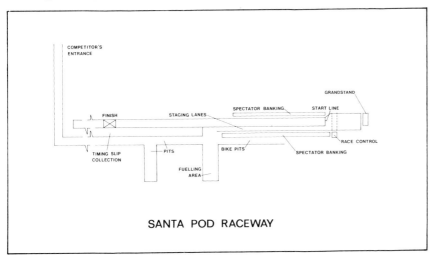

SANTA POD RACEWAY

THE NATIONAL DRAG RACING CLUB (NDRC) operates from two main venues, their newly-refabricated strip at Long Marston, in Warwickshire, and Blackbushe, in Hampshire. The Long Marston strip is on the A46, five miles south-west of Stratford-upon-Avon (don't make for the village of Long Marston, the strip is entered directly from the A46). Similarly reached directly from a trunk road, Blackbushe is on the A30 between Camberley

and Hartley Wintney, 12 miles east of Basingstoke.
NDRC Secretary
104 Essex Road
Romford
Essex
Tel: 70-60336.

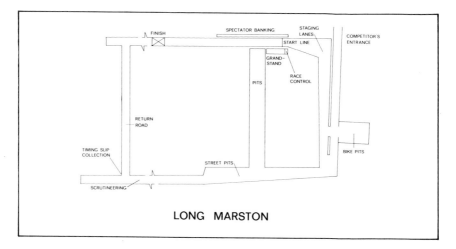

LONG MARSTON

THE PENNINE DRAG RACING CLUB's strip is a couple of miles south of the village of Melbourne, in Humberside, about 10 miles from York and vaguely south-east of that city. From intersection 37 on the M62, drive north through Howden on the B1228 and follow the PDRC's signposting. From the York bypass (A64) take the B1228 off the A1079, passing through Elvington. The strip is called the New York Dragway, and is administered by Pennine Promotions.
Pennine Promotions Office
Albert Street
Hebden Bridge
West Yorkshire.
Tel: 042284-3651

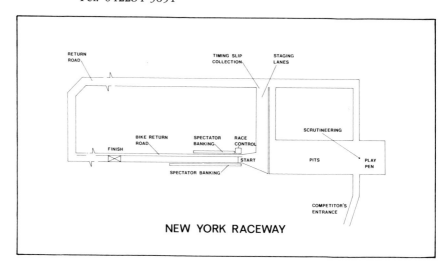

NEW YORK RACEWAY

The other address of importance for British drag racers is:
RAC Motor Sports Association
31 Belgrave Square
London SW1X 8QH.
Tel: 01-235 8601

The ACU is a division of the RAC MSA and can be reached at the Belgrave Square address.

American addresses:

American Hot Rod Association
Suite 2
4520 Madison Avenue
Kansas City
Missouri.

International Hot Rod Association
PO Box 3029
Bristol
Tennessee 37620.

National Hot Rod Association
10639 Riverside Drive
North Hollywood
California 91602.

United Bracket Racers Association
55 East Village of Stoney Run
Maple Shade
New Jersey 08052.

United Drag Racers Association
3425 Landstrom Road
Rockford
Illinois 61107.

Professional Racers Organization
PO Box 8
Seffner
Florida 33584.

SPECIALIST SUPPLIERS

A list of folk worth knowing. It doesn't include everyone, but there should be at least one guy out of this number who can provide the parts or service you need. We haven't bothered including the people who would paint your racer; that is better served by the customizing chappies, and there are so many of them. Information like that you can get from the custom magazines or *The Complete Customiser* (Sphere). The information in brackets after each business name is a generalization of the service offered.

American Parts Centre (US car parts and performance bits)
403 Tong Street, Bradford, West Yorkshire.
Tel: 0274-684565

American Autoparts (US car parts, badges, books)
77 Manor Road, Wallington, Surrey.
Tel: 01-647 4471

Americar (US bits and performance parts)
352 Southchurch Road, Southend-On-Sea, Essex.
Tel: 0702-67217

Allard PAO (Turbos and superchargers)
Newport Street, Swindon, Wiltshire.
Tel: 0793-20433

Custom Maid (US bits and V8 performance parts)
323 High Road, Ilford, Essex.
Tel: 01-553 4463

Devon Mouldings (Glass-fibre mouldings)
Heron Road, Southon Industrial Estate, Exeter, Devon.
Tel: 0392-50970

Super Power USA (American parts and performance work)
Wakefield Road, Swillington, Nr Leeds.
Tel: 0532-870111

Gary's Shack (US car parts and work)
62 Battersea High Street, London SW11.
Tel: 01-228 6612

Hatton Enterprises (Nitrous oxide kits and turbochargers)
Langwood House, Epsom Road, Ashstead, Surrey.
Tel: 27-72755

Janspeed Engineering (Turbochargers)
Southampton Road, Salisbury, Wiltshire.
Tel: 0722-6955

Mako Prototype Engineering (Glass-fibre panels)
Quarry Lane, Chichester, Sussex.
Tel: 0243-81651

Mike the Pipe (Headers and exhausts)
128 Stanley Park Road, Wallington, Surrey.
Tel: 01-669 1719

Piper RDA (Fuel injection)
Wixenford Farm, Colesdown Hill, Billacombe, Plymouth, Devon.
Tel: 0752-46214

Slick Tricks Racing (General performance work)
191A-193 Stanstead Road, Forest Hill, London SE23.
Tel: 01-291 2402

Russell Performance Products (Racing components)
140 Sandy Lane, Camp Hill, Birmingham.
Tel: 021-772 1994

John Woolfe Racing (US engine parts and performance bits)
Elms Industrial Estate, Shuttleworth Road, Bedford.
Tel: 0234-841829

Rodley Motors (American car parts)
26 East Parade, Bradford.
Tel: 0274-29425

Muscle City (Performance bits and V8 equipment)
678 Pershore Road, Selly Park, Birmingham.
Tel: 021-472 2798

Southern Muscle (Performance bits and V8 equipment)
520-522 Forest Road, Walthamstow, London E17.

Pete & Mart's (V8 performance parts)
85 Ballard's Lane, Finchley, London N3.
Tel: 01-346 3349

Howe Exhausts And Cams (Manifolds, carbs, etc)
Rear Hollyville Cafe, Main Road, West Kingsdown, Kent.
Tel: 047845-2347

Bosworth Tools Ltd (Specialist grinding and machining)
Market Bosworth, Leicestershire.
Tel: 0455-291216

SRU Autos (General speed equipment)
229 Chertsey Road, Addlestone, Surrey.
Tel: 09328-62556

Shadow Racing (Wheels and slicks)
28A Baker Street, Reading, Berkshire.
Tel: 0734-594711

G Max Research (Racing fuels)
8 Tate Road, Sutton, Surrey.
Tel: 01-642 8971

Dennis Priddle Racing (Engineering work, complete cars)
Goldcroft, Yeovil, Somerset.
Tel: 0935-6479

Coil Springs (Springs made to order)
Staniforth Road Service Station, Staniforth Road, Sheffield 9.
Tel: 0742-442676

Fibreglass Repairs (FGR) (All glass-fibre work and complete bodies)
98 Martins Road, Shortlands, Bromley, Kent.
Tel: 01-464 5445

Race Engine Components
2 Roebuck Lane, West Bromwich, West Midlands.
Tel: 021-553 1103

Custom Fastners (Bolts, screws, etc, and polishing)
Unit 32M, Heming Road, Washford Industrial Estate, Redditch, Worcestershire.
Tel: 0527-23772

Automatic Transmission Parts
Rugeley Road, Hednesford, Staffordshire.
Tel: 05438-5346

Hyperformance (Specialist fabrication, engine work, tuning)
65 Garman Road, Tottenham, London N17.
Tel: 01-450 5146

Pickford Axle Exchange (Rear axle and diff work)
84 Nunhead Grove, London SE15.
Tel: 01-732 9506

GDS Exhausts (Specialist exhaust applications)
53A Bridge Street, Brackley, Northants.
Tel: 0280-702510

STS Aley Bars (Roll cages)
London Road, Sawston, Cambridge.
Tel: 0223-832575

Tony Beadle Engineering (General engineering work and chassis)
25 Pendell Avenue, Harlington, Middlesex.
Tel: 01 897 3253

Fibreglass Applications (Glass-fibre work and engineering)
173 Chemical Road, West Wilts Trading Estate, Westbury, Wiltshire.
Tel: 0373-864359

Denis Gregory Engineering (Racing engine work)
70 Willoughby Road, Harpenden, Herts.
Tel: 05827-64494

Autopower Services (Race engineering)
South March, Long March Industrial Estate, Daventry, Northants.
Tel: 03272-76161

The Village Bike Shop (General bike work)
103A Manchester Road, Walkden, Manchester.
Tel: 061-790 2828

Maitland Racing (Bike engine parts)
17 Southampton Road, London NW5.
Tel: 01-485 0473

Johnson Engineering (Bike engine work)
Unit 7, Pontiac Works, Fernbank Road, Ascot, Berkshire.
Tel: 03447-5000

Brockliss Motorcycles (Bike engine parts)
Brockley Road, London SE4.
Tel: 01-691 5718

Uncle Bunt's Chop Shop (Bike frames for dragging)
Frogs Island Sawmills, Brightwell, Wallingford, Oxfordshire.
Tel: 0491-37666